IN
CONVER

IN
CONVERSATION

Published in Great Britain in 2001 by
Azure
1 Marylebone Road
London NW1 4DU

British Library Cataloguing-in-Publication Data

A catalogue record for this book is available from
the British Library

ISBN 1-902694-18-X

Typeset by Pioneer Associates, Perthshire
Printed in Great Britain by
Omnia Books, Bishopbriggs, Glasgow

CONTENTS

FOREWORD

The interviews all first appeared in Third Way *magazine (see page 120).*

Conversations with the famous and the powerful – or do we just mean celebrity interviews? – are a staple of the media today. From *Smash Hits* to the *Financial Times*, editors are eager to tantalize readers with the words of 'the people who matter'. Access is everything in our society, and if you will never yourself get to meet Britney Spears or Gordon Brown, at least you can overhear them in print. At any rate, that seems to be the theory.

Yet all too often what we are treated to is not so much the opinions of the movers and shakers as the interviewers' opinion of *them*. In many cases, interviews in print degenerate into an exercise in entertainment at their subjects' expense, with their words (and often their mannerisms too) used merely as raw material for a piece designed primarily to amuse the reader. Oftentimes, the interviewer themself becomes a celebrity, and the primary aim of the piece seems to be to advertise their own wisdom, insight and wit.

The nine interviews contained in this book represent a very different approach. They take it for granted that the values and principles of the people who form opinion and help to shape society in this country really do matter, and so they try to engage with them properly. Rigorous without being rude – or, if you prefer, respectful but not uncritical – they are presented as question and answer so that the reader can 'hear' more or less exactly what the subject said, and even the tone of voice in which they said it. As Susan

Howatch remarked when she saw the proofs of her interview, 'What a pleasure to find such accuracy! That is so rare.'

And so these interviews also deliver a very different response. People become guarded if they think their opinions are being solicited only so that others can find some sensation or fault in them, and it has become unusual for public figures to talk frankly to the press about their private lives and their personal beliefs and ideals. Instead, they offer calculated soundbites and stage-managed photo opportunities, which only make the public cynical. In contrast, the openness of the men and women in this book – and of the seventysomething other artists, writers, politicians, scientists, religious leaders and others who have given interviews to *Third Way* over the last eight years – is a measure of their appreciation of the way their views were being honestly sought and would be faithfully repeated.

Huw Spanner
Publisher, *Third Way*

BUILDING THE COMMON GOOD

Helen Hayes and Brian Draper talk to
the visionary international architect
Lord Rogers

**One definition of great art is that it changes people.
Do you think the same is true of great buildings?**

I think that beauty generally moves the spirit. People are
usually happy in beautiful places. The classic Georgian terrace
house is only 15 feet wide and it was actually often rather a
cheap building comparatively, but it now has a value . . . I'm
not saying that capital value equals success, but the fact that
there is such a demand for them tells you something.

Do you know those wonderful Victorian or Edwardian
developments – I love them deeply – where you have a little
garden in front and a little garden at the back and then
you have a private space which is public to all the estate,
with 200 houses around it? It's fantastic, because children
can play in safety in that space, without fear of people
wandering in.

And then the Georgian squares . . . The reason Belgravia
is so successful is the trees. You probably can't separate their
environmental impact from the beauty of the houses.
Florence, where I come from, is pretty good, too.

What buildings or public spaces move you most?

It is not a place, but I love the *passeggiata*, where the Italians
and the Spanish walk at six o'clock in the evening and the
ladies look at the men and the men look at the ladies. You
dress a little bit – but that doesn't matter: it's the whole

idea of a parade, of social exchange. You're now beginning to see it in London.

There are little spaces that can be equally wonderful. The little church behind St Paul's in Covent Garden is an example. When all hell is breaking out around, you can go into the churchyard. It's just as interesting as the other, rowdy side of Covent Garden – more so in some ways. Having said how important community is, I think it's also very important that we have places where we can be isolated. Where you can sit under a tree. In Britain, our parks are second to none.

Cities are for the meeting of people – of strangers as well as friends. The street should be a human place, a civic place

Is there a spiritual dimension to architecture and urban design?

It should have, but probably everything should have. The built environment is a primary element in our civic society. The ancient oath when the Athenians were made citizens went along the lines of 'I shall leave the city more beautiful than it was when I entered it' – 'beautiful' not just in an aesthetic sense but in the sense of 'more liveable', if you like.

Cities are for the meeting of people: for the meeting of strangers as well as friends. The street is where we tend to meet most people, and it should be a human place, a civic place. The doorstep is very important, and the green and so on.

I became an architect because I was interested both in art and in social and political problems. Architecture has the potential to link the two.

When you are designing a building, are you thinking of people, or of making a work of art?

I don't think you start with the idea of a work of art. You start with pretty basic things like square metres and costs and people's needs – including spiritual needs, if you like, or needs from the heart; and you put all this in a melting-pot and it slowly builds up. I have doubts about that sudden creative moment. If it happens to me, it is usually at three in the morning and I know I've drunk too much the next day. Of course, you do have insights, on the plane as easily as at the work table, and you can have small jumps of imagination – and that's very critical, the imagination. But it mustn't just lead . . . It can't lead, because you're not an abstract artist.

In a way, I prefer the process to the end. I always have. I'm slightly lost when the end arrives. I feel – I don't know about let down, but I want to get on to the next one. I'm not saying I won't ever go back – and sometimes you're even invited back! But I prefer the next challenge. People say, 'You're lucky. Your buildings will be around for a long time,' but that's certainly not the reason I do it for. My wife's a chef. I see very little difference between her cooking a great meal, which you eat straightaway, and me building Lloyd's. They're both acts of the imagination.

You don't think, 'People may be looking at this in two hundred years' time'?

I can't pretend that I have no awareness of history, if you want to put it that way: I enjoy going to see beautiful buildings, whether by Inigo Jones or by Norman Foster. But I don't think I see my buildings in the same way. You don't deal with it, perhaps, because you can't. I don't know if that makes sense.

What would your more civic city look like?

Copenhagen has done amazing studies – the Danish are rather good at them – which show that over the last 30 years, let's say, there has been a threefold increase of people spending time in the street – which is a lot to do with things like pedestrianization, having cafés facing south, having outside heaters, having places which are safe and so on.

These studies also show that if you spend time in the street you are much more likely to talk to each other. There's a study that shows three streets in the same block in San Francisco, one with heavy traffic, one with medium traffic and one with low traffic; and – it's pretty obvious – roughly ten times as many people know each other in the street where there is low traffic than in the busy street.

Also, people lived in the quiet street for something like 50 per cent longer than in the busy street, for an average of 12 years rather than eight.

Finally, one of the most horrific statistics I have is that in 1971 80 per cent of eight and nine-year-old children walked to school. In 1999, 10 per cent did. Germany hasn't had that jump: they have gone from 80 to 70 per cent, but not to 10.

Congestion is probably one of the minor problems. We are talking about friendship, because a car is basically an armoured car: you drive from door to door, you don't meet other parents, or other children. As a terrible student, the only fun I used to have was walking home from school with my friends, kicking a ball or picking blackberries or whatever.

So, the ideal situation is, yes, the hamlet, the village, the neighbourhood. If you want the reverse, I have been studying Manchester. East Manchester, which is about a fifth of what was almost certainly one of the richest cities in the world, has lost 50 per cent of its population since the war, and 80 per cent since the First World War. It's totally fragmented.

Talk about the city of the night! This is it. Obviously, there's no community feeling; obviously, it is a place of fear. And the only people left there are the people who really are so poor they can't move out. I am not blaming the people: I'm blaming the state we find ourselves in. The gap between poor and rich in England is the greatest in Europe.

How do you regenerate the inner city without displacing the poor and creating something exclusive?
The only way you're going to get to evade that market pressure is for the Government to stipulate that a percentage of buildings – or, it might be better, a percentage of people – must receive financial aid. The only alternative is to

keep these areas permanently poor, and that's an impossible situation.

I do think there is a serious problem of ghettoization, I have to say, whether it's poor or rich. All countries suffer, but some places are much worse. We played a game in Holland, when I went with the Urban Task Force, of trying to guess on the best estates which is private and which is social housing. Well, you can't. In this country, you know from one glance which is social housing. The trick is that it has to be so integrated that you don't see it.

Do you think there is a role for churches and faith communities in urban regeneration?

I think there is a role for any form of entrepreneurialism, and I see the church in those terms. I have to quickly say I'm not religious. It's to do with people meeting with a common idea which fosters citizenship or a civic pride. I don't mind terribly where it comes from, but the fostering of those ideas is critical for our society.

How does your understanding of human nature affect your architecture?

It's the basis of what we do, to try and understand human nature – including market pressure. And we do misread situations. We certainly got it wrong with the high rise, there's no question about that.

I think the problem was not the high rise per se. It's partly the way we built them, partly the way we managed them, partly that we only gave them to the poor. If you come from the Continent, the chances are you live in an apartment on the sixth floor – or, in the States, the 16th floor. But those blocks have a concierge and that's a very important part of it, that there is someone (ideally, a family) down there who knows if somebody's in trouble on the 33rd floor. So, there's a community there.

We got it all wrong. Central government made the decisions, massive estates were built and people were moved.

> My wife is a chef. I see very little difference between her cooking a great meal and me building Lloyd's. They're both acts of the imagination

Not neighbourhoods, just people. If you take families out of their neighbourhoods, so that the whole kinship structure is eroded, and then force them onto the 20th floor, you can hardly be surprised if there are social problems.

In Holland, they accepted that it would be less fast but they gave it to the control of the neighbourhoods, who selected the architects, the sociologists, the doctors, whatever. Five to ten thousand people, more or less, would come together to create a housing association. I'm not saying they got it all right – they've got problems, too – but overall they avoided the worst of our problems.

Architects were certainly partly responsible: we sold a dream which wasn't suited to the public demand. But I think there has been a reaction which is also illogical, because individualization means there are people who really enjoy living up high. Students, for instance, often have no objection to living off the ground, and why should they? They have great views and the air is probably cleaner. Old people as well, strangely enough.

How have you coped with the conservatism of your adopted country?

I think it's changing amazingly. If I look at London – if I don't look at the poorer areas (and, of course, one has to – and four of the ten poorest boroughs in England are in fact in London) – overall, I have never seen the populace so easy with its city.

As an example, the only espresso machine ten years or so ago in London was in Soho. Now round where I live there are almost too many. I'm amazed. I'm using that as an index of street life. The whole British thing, which used to shock me (putting my foreigner's hat on), was that everything was inward-looking: in the pub, you had to be male and working-class, in the club you had to be posh and pay the dues. But now the pub has become the coffee place, and the clubs are probably doing not so well, and people are meeting each other in the street, people are talking, in Covent Garden, Soho . . .

OK, there are still battles between people and traffic, it's still polluted, there are still a lot of problems – and, as I said, other cities are suffering more; but there is a return to the centre. Nearly all the major cities now are seeing an increase in the number of people – from nearly zero in the centres of Birmingham, Manchester and so on, I have to say – but there are thousands now, and they are moving into the old buildings as well as into new ones.

Visually, I think the British (or the English, who are rather different) suffer greatly from the shock of the new; but internationalization is softening that, too. The South Bank is the biggest change I've seen in my lifetime. When you walk from Battersea Park to the Design Museum to the new Tate to the Globe – it's fantastic. People are there all the time – and are coming there from all over the world, so again we're becoming much less isolated.

I know, of course, as we read in the papers, we are still very frightened of foreigners, and especially immigrants. But it's a lot, lot better than it was.

Even if we are being selfish, we still can't say, 'I'm all right, Jack' because the state of the Third World, say, does impact us

The proposals the Urban Task Force has made require significant changes in the way we live. You are asking the British to give up their gardens front and back, for example. Do you think that is achievable?

That's complicated. First of all, I'm not convinced about this tradition. I think it was forced by the Industrial Revolution (by which I mean something that went on until a few years ago). It was so unpleasant in cities, especially in the nineteenth century, that anyone who could get out did. In 1841, the life expectancy of a working person in the city was less than 20 years. Of course you'd get out if you could.

Before that, Georgian cities were fantastic, probably the greatest in the civilized world (or whatever you like to call it). Of course, industry made cities, because everyone came for the money and the work; but it also, in a sense, destroyed the civic pride and citizenship which is what, as I see it, cities are for.

So, I don't really believe that the English are enamoured of their gardens quite so much as they hate the appalling state of their cities. I'm not a politician, but I think that if you offered them the modern equivalent to a beautiful Georgian city, people would go there – especially if you controlled the traffic.

I also think that some immense changes are happening. I think there are three driving principles, which have become understandable only in the last few decades. One is the environmental revolution, a sudden knowledge that ecology cannot be ignored. We have to have sustainability, which is a long-term vision about what we do with our earth.

That consciousness just didn't exist when I was young. Looking back, I think that going into space changed our vision of our responsibility outside our little village or town or nation to a global consciousness of what is going on and its impact on us. So, even if we are being selfish we still can't say, 'I'm all right, Jack,' because the state of the Third World, say, does impact us.

Second, the information network has given us the possibility of clean energy. The brain is much cleaner than brawn, if you like, and therefore we don't need to pollute. And, of course, that network allows us to look not just at the town and the nation but at the regions, at Europe, at the globe.

And, third, just over a hundred years ago in the cities, life expectancy was about 40. I read the other day that the average lifespan in Japan for women is now 83. Both my mother and my wife's mother are in their late eighties and are going strong. My grandchildren could live to 100. Longevity means changing life-patterns, fewer children: 1.7 in England, 1.2 in Italy and Spain (in Catholic countries – fascinating). My grandparents had eight children, my great-grandparents probably had more.

Society is becoming individualized, which is both good and bad. The figure we have from the Government is that, of the four million new dwellings we need over the next 20 years, 80 per cent are so-called single-person dwellings. We've suddenly gone from 10 per cent of the nation living in apartments to 20 per cent over a very short period, because if you're single, or you're cohabiting, you probably want to live in a city whether you're 30 or 65. Do you really want to live with a big garden out in suburbia?

Why is individualization both good and bad?
Well, the bad is that there's less to drive the family together, because in a sense children were the main reason for most people to stay together. If you're going to have one-point-something children – I have five boys, but then there are a lot of other people making up for my antisocial behaviour – that is probably part of the reason for the divorce rate.

I'm not at all convinced that that form of fragmentation is bad. You could see it as empowering society to go the 'third way' – in other words, neither business nor government but voluntary work and so on. A hundred years ago, the woman had 12 children and when the last one left she dropped dead, more or less. The man worked in a mine and when he retired at 60 he probably had three or four years and then he dropped dead. We now have 30 years.

I think this offers a lot of good things – as long as we use that free time in a broader, social way. Which doesn't mean it shouldn't be enjoyable.

Do you think that architecture has a moral as well as a spiritual dimension?
I think it does, a moral and ethical dimension.

Does that mean that good people are good designers? No, it doesn't. It doesn't work like that. But morality may not make good designers but it makes good people, which is probably more important – using 'good' in a very broad sense.

Of course, if you have limited vision, limited imagination, and you have no consciousness, that definitely can make you a bad designer, or a bad artist. The trouble is, you also come across these questions – you know, was Ezra Pound a Fascist, and does it make his poetry worse? Caravaggio was not a nice person, if you met him on a dark night, yet he was perhaps the Romans' greatest painter – and his religious paintings are still amazing.

I think my wife would disagree with me – she does actually feel much more that the work expresses the nature of the individual. But certainly, taking it the other way round, a lot of bad architecture is done by people who have no social consciousness.

A lot of bad architecture is big and bombastic, and designed to intimidate the individual . . .

I think a lack of consciousness is the main problem – in other words, lack of understanding of appropriateness. There are appropriate uses of large spaces where the individual feels wonderful. Chartres Cathedral is fantastic.

On the other hand, it seems to me questionable whether a building designed for Mammon should look like a cathedral. There is a certain point where one would call it Fascist. Whether that's the right word I don't know, but Fascist buildings often have no scale, which is not so much about size as about detail. What makes the Gothic cathedral so understandable is that it's full of human details, the way it breaks down so that even though the scale is tremendous, it's actually related to the little man or woman down there.

Why do you think that non-religious people can be moved when they go into Gothic cathedrals?

Because they're spiritual. I prefer the word 'spiritual' – I think everybody has a spirit. We may not all have the same belief, but I don't think in the end it matters much whether you are from Saudi Arabia, say, or an Eskimo: if you go into York Minster, I'm sure you will be just as moved.

Equally, religious people feel moved when they go into the church at Ronchamp (which I think is a wonderful, wonderful building), which was designed by Le Corbusier. He wasn't religious but I think he was spiritual, and I think it is possible to express that without actually belonging to a faith.

What do you think is the equivalent to the cathedral for this millennium? No doubt you've been asked that many times before.

I'm not sure I have, actually. I'll have to think . . . It is probably something like the town square.

It's a very interesting question, because the thing about the cathedral is that it works empty and full, in bad or good weather, unlike a square . . . I should ask you. Do you think it has to be a church?

It's civic pride as well, isn't it, that drives those cathedrals and I think it's civic pride we're talking about, and that can be a big space or a small space. If you go to a Buddhist shrine – you know, where you have just wood and paper, often just enclosing a space, they are equally spiritual. It probably is to do with proportion more than anything else.

I think you can be moved under a tree, by the way. It can be anything, it can happen anywhere.

What do you put your faith in?

People. What do I put my faith in? Relationships . . .

I think we have a social responsibility. Especially people like ourselves, who happen to be more fortunate than others, have a duty. I feel that very strongly. There is that sense that, but for a little chance, there go I . . . There's a lot of luck in this game, to put it mildly, and therefore one should share that luck, I suppose, and that's a sort of faith. And I believe that you can improve things.

To say the opposite of [Margaret] Thatcher, it's all about society. It's all about relationships, it's all about the feeling of being part of a community, of friendship in the simplest

What do I put my faith in? People

terms – and also the responsibility that goes beyond us as individuals to the ecology, the globe and everything else.

BIOGRAPHY

Richard Rogers was born in Florence in 1933. He studied at the Architectural Association in London from 1954 to 1959, and in 1962 took a master's degree at Yale University, where he was a Fulbright and Yale Scholar.

In 1963, he formed Team 4 with Norman Foster, Su Rogers and Wendy Foster, working chiefly on residential projects. Subsequent collaborations with Su Rogers and Renzo Piano culminated in the foundation of the Richard Rogers Partnership in 1977.

His most famous buildings are the Centre Georges Pompidou in Paris (1971–77), which he designed with Piano, the headquarters of Lloyd's of London (1978–86) and the Millennium Dome (1996–99). He 'masterplanned' the development of the Royal Docks in London (1984–86), Potsdamer Platz in Berlin (1991–92), Shanghai's Pu Dong financial district (1992) and the Greenwich Peninsula site of the Dome (1997 to date).

Other buildings he has designed include the headquarters of PA Technology in Cambridge (1975–85) and in Princeton in the United States (1982–85), Marseille Airport (1989–92), the Kabuki-Cho Tower in Tokyo (1987–93), the Channel 4 HQ in London (1991–94), the European Court of Human Rights in Strasbourg (1989–95), the VR Techno offices and laboratories in Gifu in Japan (1993–98), the Law Courts in Bordeaux (1993–99), a major office block in London commissioned originally by Daiwa Europe (1990–99) and, in the City, the new HQ for Lloyd's Register of Shipping (1995–2000).

His plans for the centre of London were exhibited in the Royal Academy in 1986, alongside those of Norman Foster and James Stirling.

He is currently masterplanning Heathrow Airport's Terminal 5, Piana di Castello in Florence and the ParcBIT development in Majorca. The partnership has also won international competitions to design new law courts in Antwerp and the National Assembly for Wales in Cardiff.

In 1998, he was asked by the Government to chair its Urban Task Force. Their report, *Towards an Urban Renaissance*, led to the Government's Urban White Paper, responding to the UTF recommendations.

He has taught at the Architectural Association, the Universities of Cambridge and Yale and University College, Los Angeles. In 1995, he gave the BBC Reith Lectures, on the theme of 'Cities for a Small Planet', which were subsequently published under that title.

Richard Rogers was chair of the Tate Gallery from 1981 to 1989, and deputy chair of the Arts Council of England from 1994 to 1997. He is a member of the UN Architects' Committee, a trustee of London First and a UK director of Médecins du Monde, and chairs both the Architecture Foundation and the National Tenants Resource Centre. He is also patron of the Society of Black Architects.

His publications include *Architecture: A Modern View* (1990) and *A New London* (1992) with Mark Fisher. He has been the subject of biographies by Bryan Appleyard and Kenneth Powell and of studies by Deyan Sudjic and Richard Burdett. The first of a three-volume series by Powell entitled *Richard Rogers: Complete Works* was published in 1999. His 1995 BBC Reith Lecture series, entitled *Cities for a Small Planet*, addressed some of the environmental and social problems of today's cities, and discussed ways in which architects and planners can act together to curb the disintegration of urban life, and enhance sustainability. These lecture texts were published in book form the following year by Faber and Faber. The book has since been translated into Spanish, Catalan and Italian. Further editions in French, German and Japanese are currently under way. Its sequel, *Cities for a Small Country* (co-authored by Professor Anne Power,

London School of Economics) was published in October 2000.

He was elected to the Royal Academy in 1984. He is also an academician of the International Academy of Architecture and a member of l'Academie d'Architecture. He is an honorary fellow of Cardiff University, and holds honorary doctorates from the Royal College of Arts, the Universities of Bath, North London, the South Bank and Westminster and the Czech Technical University in Prague.

The many international awards he has received include the Gold Medal of the Royal Institute of British Architects in 1985 and the Thomas Jefferson Memorial Foundation Medal in 1999. In 1986, he was appointed a Chevalier de la Légion d'Honneur. He was awarded the prestigious Praemium Imperiale in 2000.

He was knighted in 1991 and was created a life peer in 1996, taking the title of The Lord Rogers of Riverside.

Richard Rogers has been married twice, and has five sons.

This interview was conducted in the offices of the Richard Rogers Partnership in west London on 31 March 2000.

At the time of the interview Brian Draper was editor of *Third Way*. He now lectures in contemporary culture at the London Institute for Contemporary Christianity. His first book, *Refreshing Worship*, co-written with Kevin Draper, was published by Bible Reading Fellowship in 2000.

Helen Hayes is a director of the urban regeneration consultancy Town Centres. She has a master's degree in social policy from the London School of Economics and Political Science.

SOME STRAIGHT ANSWERS

Steve Turner talks to the doyen of
BBC Radio 1 and star of Radio 4
John Peel OBE

You are, very possibly, even more celebrated now as the presenter of BBC Radio 4's Home Truths than as a DJ on Radio 1. Was it your idea?

Not at all. I had done a magazine programme on Radio 4 called *Offspring* which was quite successful. When James Boyle arrived [as the Controller of Radio 4], I was asked if I'd like to do a one-hour programme on Saturday morning. I did it because I was flattered to be asked and also because the programme it replaced was about sport, which used to irritate me, and had particularly awful theme music.

Some people have criticized you for going soft.

For some reason, the *Guardian* and the *Observer* rather turned on me. There was a fantastically hysterical piece by Julie Burchill which accused me of operating a racist music policy and being a child molester. It was really very unpleasant. But what do you do? If you make a fuss and consult lawyers, it just draws attention, which is what they want.

Did you think you were entering strange territory by doing a programme that dealt with family matters?

Not really. I like being a dad and a husband. I found that doing *Offspring* helped me to sort out some of my own thinking about life and to come to terms with things that had bothered me growing up.

I really believed in all of that flower-power stuff, but over a period of time I became quite disenchanted with it all. It seemed in the end so amazingly selfish

My dad was away fighting the war until I was six, and then I was packed off to a boarding school. He lived until I was in my late twenties and I think was a very nice man, but I never really knew him terribly well. I've had a lot of trouble sorting out in my head my relationship with my dad, which was based almost entirely on my asking him for money and him, very reluctantly, giving it to me. I was a great disappointment to him and I was conscious of that.

Do you regret some of your early failures?

It's a very obvious thing that, if you like doing what you do and being where you are, you have reached that point as much as a result of your failures as of your successes.

If I had succeeded at school, I would have been a very different person to the one I am now. I could have been an accountant in Cheshire. When I grew up, there weren't many options open to you. If you were successful in everything, you went from school to university and into the family business or the armed services. You only had options if you failed. (I'd like to pretend that I had worked this out, but it wasn't something I thought about at the time.)

Did there come a time when you were able to sort out your feelings towards your parents?

Yes. There was a key moment when, instead of feeling sorry for myself, I felt it was more appropriate to feel sorry for them. It was triggered by a TV programme which took me back to Anglesey, where I had a holiday in 1945 or 1946. My mother rented a large house there. One day my brother and I dashed out to see a motorcycle pass by and, instead of going by, it turned into the driveway. I told my mother that there was a funny-looking man outside and she looked out and said, 'It's your father.' It was the first time I had seen him.

As I recounted this on TV, standing on the actual spot where it happened, I could feel something almost physical coming up through my body. I thought it was a heart attack.

It came right up into my throat and then I started howling and fell to the ground. It was a very traumatic moment. That's what started me thinking about what it must have been like for my dad rather than what it was like for me.

My brother Alan, who is seven years younger than me, has breakfast with me once a week and, whatever we start talking about, we always end up talking about our dad.

Did you think of yourself as a potential family man in the Sixties?

Not really. I lived in the States from 1960 until 1967 and I got married there to a 15-year-old girl – which is where Julie Burchill got her idea of me being a child abuser. It was perfectly legal but obviously disastrous for me and even more disastrous for her. She had a lot of growing up to do. She had an absolutely awful life (she's dead now). She married three other people after me and had a lot of children that went into care. We were married for three or four years.

After we had been apart for a year or two, I met Sheila. When we got married, we weren't thinking about having children at all. I was rather opposed to the idea. We bought a cottage in East Anglia (where we still live) and at night, before we went to sleep, Sheila would read me Richmal Crompton's William stories, which I'd never read before. Gradually, we decided how nice it would be to have our own William. She stopped taking the Pill, and we had children every two years until we had got four. We'd have had more, actually, if she hadn't got quite seriously ill with the last one.

You came to prominence at a time when family life was not considered very appealing.

During the hippy period, people obviously didn't think in terms of children – they only thought in terms of themselves. I really believed in all of that flower-power stuff. I really did. People have told me subsequently that I was seen as rather a comic figure because of that. But over a period of time I became quite disenchanted with it all. It seemed in the end so selfish, because it was all based on the principle of dropping out of society, without consideration for the vast majority of people who had never been given the opportunity of dropping in.

Even by the end of the Sixties I began to think it was amazingly selfish. I wasn't very much into drugs and things because they made me feel sick, which obviously wasn't what you were supposed to experience. There was a lot of shagging going on, but even that began to pall after a while. We were supposed to be considering other people and yet we were so exploitative of women. *Oz*, in particular, and *International Times* had an attitude towards women that was fairly appalling. At worst, they were just sex slaves, in effect.

I found myself having it off with a go-go girl on the tiled floor of a men's toilet at Portsmouth City Hall and I just thought, 'Actually, this is about as low as you can go.' After that, I started to try and treat people with more respect. There were a lot of important moral lessons learnt along the way.

Where did you get the values from which helped you to judge the failings of the counterculture?

A good question. I don't know. My family wasn't religious. My dad, bless him, had memorized huge chunks of the Old Testament at some stage in his life and was given to quoting them, but he wasn't a believer particularly. I think he relished the Bible for its language – as I do. I read the Bible, but I'm not religious.

Every day?

Good Lord, no. Just every once in a while. Because of the language of the King James Version. There's a lot of good stuff in there. Somewhere there's a bit about those whom the Lord is displeased with and they are referred to as 'companions to owls'. I find that well nigh irresistible.

Have you ever been a religious person?

At one stage I did think about going into the church, but that was only from despair when leaving school and thinking, 'What the hell am I going to do?' The church seemed a not unreasonable option.

The man who influenced me most in my life was my housemaster at school, R. H. J. Brooke, who in retirement went into the church. He was an extraordinary man. I was bottom of the school in my first term, and just a constant pain. I wasn't some James Dean figure: I was just stupid and forgetful. I drifted around in a trance – there was a lot of pressure to get me thrown out. When he became my form master in the third year, I came top. He persuaded me that learning stuff was worthwhile.

He was a very moral man, and also powerfully eccentric, which I liked. He was the sort of person that, subconsciously, you knew you'd like to be like.

Would you describe yourself as agnostic or atheist?

I don't know, really. If I believed in a god, it would be a rather vengeful and capricious old fellow lurking in the roof of a rather nice old building waiting to zap you for some imagined crime, rather than a Cliff Richard type of god who lets you beat him at table tennis.

My enthusiasm for organized religion evaporated pretty early on. At my prep school, the people responsible for my spiritual welfare were sadists and paedophiles. At Shrewsbury, we used to get beaten for being late for chapel, which I used to think ran rather counter to the spirit of Christian forgiveness. I like the language – I like the singing, really – but I don't like the things people do in the name of religion. So often it is used as a club with which to bully other people.

My own creed, such as it is, is the very obvious one of 'Do as you would be done by.' I would always tell the children: 'Treat other people as you would like them to treat you.' But that doesn't really fall into any established religious observation.

I do like going into churches and cathedrals because, although I don't believe in the things that the people who built them believed in, I'm impressed by the intensity of their beliefs. These buildings are quite literally awe-inspiring – a tangible expression of a belief that often takes a more aggressive and destructive form. I think in religious art you get the best of religion. Human frailty is eradicated.

Do Christian bands send you tapes?

They don't advertise themselves as such. There is a non-specific spirituality in a lot of music anyway.

There was a fellow called Norman somebody...

Larry Norman?

Yes. He seemed like a decent fellow and his records weren't too bad; but most Christian rock is awful.

One of the qualities with which people most strongly associate you is integrity.

I don't know what people mean by 'integrity'. I've always found it easier to tell the truth because that way you don't have to remember what you've said. So, for purely practical reasons it is the best thing.

You also always seem to be deeply interested in the things you are involved with.

It's like the honesty thing: it's just easier to do that. If bagpipe music suddenly became terrifically popular, I couldn't fake an immense interest. But there is always enough going on. At the moment, there is more happening than ever to keep me interested.

My housemaster, Brooke, said in one of his reports: 'The only hope I can see for this boy is that he devises some way of earning a living from his love of records and his enthusiasm for writing enormously long and very tedious essays.' Very perceptive. I do find writing my column for the *Radio Times* and the scripts for *Home Truths* very therapeutic.

> I've always found it easier to tell the truth because that way you don't have to remember what you've said

In a sense, you are paid just to be John Peel.

Yes. What a wonderful thing! I'm paid quite well to do the things I would want to do anyway. People say, 'What would you like to do next?' and I say I just want to go on doing what I'm doing. In this respect, I'm fantastically lucky. Most people don't get to do what they would really like to do in life.

You've also managed to stay cool for a long time.

I think that's just to do with being boringly straight. The only times I get letters of complaint are when I do voiceovers for commercials and people think I've compromised myself. I'm certainly not a saint, but I do try and advertise things I actually use. I did have a pension with Equitable Life, for example.

I once did one for a lawn treatment that contained something that had been banned under the terms of the Geneva Convention and I got a lot of stick for that. I have to confess that was one I had never used, but I was desperately short of money and the children had to be fed and clothed.

It's an interesting paradox that you have maintained your coolness by being unfashionably straight.

I have never thought of myself as cool. I'd love to be cool. There are cool people who work for Radio 1 and they don't think of me as being one of them, and nor do I.

I think the reason people put up with what I do is because it's not done in an attempt to be cool. I look and dress like a minicab driver and people can live with that. If I was a 60-year-old bloke who was trying to be cool, people would be alienated. I know people might say I'm being modest and self-deprecating, but I'm as vain as anyone else.

How do you manage to stay current?

There is so much going on that you're not disqualified by age from enjoying. If you're interested in literature or film,

> I have the highest percentage of listeners under the age of 16 on Radio 1. I think that is rather wonderful, when I'm old enough to be their grandfather

no one says, 'Sorry, mate, you're 60. You've got to spend the rest of your life watching Carry On films.' It just seems to me to be part of the normal human condition to be as interested in what's happening now as you are in what has already happened.

My interest in what goes into the Radio 1 programme is genuine. We have the highest percentage of listeners under the age of 16 on Radio 1. I think that is rather wonderful, when I'm old enough to be their grandfather.

How can you still be interested in what 17-year-olds are recording in their bedrooms?

It's just a rather obsessive interest, to be honest, in hearing stuff that I've not already heard. There is no logic to it.

Don't you find yourself thinking that you're hearing something for the third or fourth time around?

Yes. That's why I was never interested in Britpop: I had heard all the people they were copying. I love the thrill of discovery, and there are so many exciting and amusing things going on which come from strange sources.

I remember you once playing a tape on your show of the noise made by the road surface of the M1.

They were experimenting with different types of surface, and I used to think it would be wonderful if they could orchestrate the roads so that they played tunes as you drove over them and you could change the tempo by driving faster or slower. It was hippy nonsense, but rather entertaining.

Do you listen to the sort of records you play on your shows when you're at home?

Yes. I would listen to them anyway. One of my frustrations is that I don't actually hear many radio programmes that play records I like. There was a time when I used to listen to tapes of my own programme, but then I thought that if I was in a car crash and they found me lying there covered in blood with a tape of one of my own programmes playing they would think I was rather big-headed.

How many records do you own?

Far too many... I'm just coming up to 25,500 vinyl LPs, about 80,000 seven-inch singles and then there are CDs, tapes and 12-inch singles on top of that.

Is that one of the reasons you haven't moved?

Certainly is, actually. Also, I like where we live and I like the people who live around us, and the fact that East Anglia is unpretentious and uncomplicated.

Do your kids think you're groovy?

Goodness, no! They think I'm a complete pillock. That's what you do think about your dad up until a certain age, and then you probably develop a grudging respect.

I tend to tell my kids how I'm feeling, and sometimes that might be a bit difficult for them to cope with, or a bit unfair of me. I've made as many mistakes as the average father, if not more. There's no way you're going to get it all right. You can only hope to get it less wrong.

How will you cope when they all leave home?

I've always hated it even when they're away staying with friends, I must admit. I used to go and stare at their empty beds and look mournful. William's now away in Newcastle, Alexandra is on the south coast, Tom is studying film in Sheffield and Flossie is at home doing A-levels. When she leaves, I'm going to feel very empty.

What is so good about family life?

It's not necessarily good for everyone. It's been good for me, even given the things earlier on that didn't work out, because I've been lucky in being married to an astonishing woman and having four by-and-large really nice children.

As I often say, rather flippantly, if I died tomorrow I couldn't complain, because I've had a really good time.

Not many people from your era have had marriages that have lasted as long as yours.

No. But it took me two gos to get it right. I always say that the world would be a much better place if everyone had a Sheila in their lives. When she was very ill four years ago and very nearly died, it was like staring through the gates of hell for a couple of weeks. It was absolutely terrifying.

Did you pray?

Not in any recognizable form, I don't think. It was more born of anger.

I was on the Isle of Man when she had a brain haemorrhage. Alexandra phoned me up and I spent an unspeakable night trying to get off the island. I remember standing on the cliffs over Douglas just kind of shouting into the night with defiance. It was like, 'How dare you?'

But you didn't go back and shout 'Thank you' afterwards.

No. I felt it was the doctors who had done it.

Do you feel that *Home Truths* is tapping into something important in British culture?

In the early days of the programme, we had a woman on who had a phobia about buttons and assumed she was alone in the world, and a lot of people wrote in saying that they were frightened of buttons, too.

Also, I've found that we can take nightmarish experiences and show that they are more common than people think, and you can sense the relief. You take pressure off people.

That's rather wonderful.

Do you see the programme as an influence for good?

No, not really. That would be terribly pompous. If you start thinking like that, you then start trying to make it like that and it becomes kind of worthy.

What would you most like people to say of you?

When I die, I would like some unsympathetic journalist like Julie Burchill to try to find someone who could say, 'He took advantage of me in some way' and not to be able to find anyone. Perhaps in the Sixties I took advantage of people sexually, but not too many.

That's what I would want, really. For people to say: He didn't take advantage of other people.

BIOGRAPHY

John Peel was born John Ravenscroft in 1939 and educated at Woodlands School, Deganwy and Shrewsbury School.

After two years' National Service in the Royal Artillery, he worked briefly as a mill operative in Rochdale before moving to the United States in 1960, where he became first an office boy and subsequently a computer programmer.

In 1962, he embarked on a career as a disc jockey, working part-time for WRR in Dallas before moving on to KLMA in Oklahoma City and KMEN outside Los Angeles, among other stations. Having been born near Liverpool, he found it helpful to pretend a personal acquaintance with The Beatles.

He returned to Britain in 1967 to join the pirate station Radio London, where he presented the celebrated show *The Perfumed Garden*. He jumped ship to BBC Radio 1 for its launch later that year, establishing himself with the late-night *Top Gear*.

He started writing a weekly column for the *Radio Times* in 1993, and presented four series of *Offspring* on BBC Radio 4 (for which he won a Sony Gold Award) from 1995 to 1997. Currently, in addition to his shows on Radio 1, he presents the successful *Home Truths* programme on Saturday mornings on Radio 4.

Besides topping the 'best DJ' polls in the music press for many years, John Peel was named 'Broadcaster of the Year' at the 1993 Sony Awards, and 'Godlike Genius' by the *New Musical Express* at the 1994 Brat Awards. He has received an honorary MA from the University of East Anglia and an honorary DMus from Anglia Polytechnic.

He was created an OBE in 1998.

He has been married to Sheila since 1974.

This interview was conducted in Needles Wine Bar in London on 22 March 2000.

Steve Turner is a freelance writer and poet. His most recent book, *Wide Awake at Midnight*, is to be published shortly. Others include the biographies of Jack Kerouac and Marvin Gaye *Angelheaded Hipster* (Bloomsbury) and *Trouble Man* (Michael Joseph), and a book of poems for children, *Dad, You're Not Funny* (Lion). His rock journalism has appeared in *Rolling Stone*, *The Times*, the *NME* and *Q*.

SLIVERS OF TRUTH

Carolyn Armitage talks to novelist
Susan Howatch

Had you always wanted to be a huge success, or was your early ambition merely to be published?

I was very motivated when I was younger. I was very ambitious and wanted to have lots of money and be very successful. Why that was I don't really know: it might have been to do with being an only child.

When I was about 40, 42, I had everything I wanted and I woke up one morning and realized I was very, very miserable. And then I really began to ask myself a lot of searching questions. By serving myself I had actually made myself very unhappy. That was the beginning of my conversion.

Self-realization doesn't always accompany success. Why did it come to you?

Who knows? The Holy Spirit bloweth where it listeth. I do think that it's God that converts people. God comes to meet people and you can only run away for so long.

We don't really know what goes on in other people's minds. They might appear to be unconverted, but perhaps deep down they're engaging in all kinds of inner dialogue we know nothing about.

Had you thought about God before?

No, not really. I didn't come from a religious background. I always thought God was around somewhere, but he never seemed to have any relevance to me. I wasn't a churchgoer.

> For 2000 years Christianity has been picked over by the very best minds of every century. There is an enormous store of accumulated wisdom

But now you go to church daily.

I try to, yes. I live near Westminster Abbey and I like to go to a weekday evensong. I like evensong because it pays equal attention to all the people in the Trinity – it's not so Christocentric as the Eucharist. It even gives a salutation to St Mary with the Magnificat.

The Eucharist to me remains a complete mystery. I go to church to hear the sermon and to hear what the Bible readings are – I am very much a Protestant in many ways.

I find worship the most difficult thing of all. I find it much easier to approach God in absolute silence and absolutely alone. On the other hand, I do think one needs the framework of a church ceremony, a service. Otherwise, it's very easy to go over the top into gnosticism or some sort of spiritual arrogance. You need the discipline.

For 2000 years Christianity has been picked over by the very best minds of every century and there is an enormous store of accumulated wisdom. Just to cut yourself loose from that and say 'I don't like the churches' is actually rather feeble. The task is to explore what's been handed down, no matter how difficult worship is.

What changed after your conversion?

My first question was: What does God require of me? I wasn't at all sure he wanted me to go on writing. I thought the only way to discern the will of God was to start reading about Christianity, to find out more about God. After a while I thought perhaps I was supposed to go back to college and do a degree in theology so I could teach.

It took some months to discern God's will. Even when I had finished *Glittering Images* (which was the book that came to me during that time) I wasn't sure, and put the manuscript away in a drawer. I thought, 'Maybe this is self-indulgence.'

Then I found I had to begin the second book because it was all in my head, waiting to begin. I still wasn't sure when my agent came over from New York and said, 'Can I have a little peep?' She was very keen, and so was my British agent, and finally I thought: 'I've waited all this time and I tried to put them off and said "Oh, it's just a sort of church thing." Right, this is what I am supposed to do: to go on writing but in a very different way, on Christian themes.'

I used to write on moral themes before but on more humanist ones. I always believed in the bad getting their deserts and the good getting their rewards in a rather oblique, sophisticated way.

Wasn't it daunting to discover that God meant you to write about Christian things?

Well, I don't set out to write polemics. For me always the people come first. But if you are a Christian, by a very mysterious process what you believe in will come through.

I've found that, certainly, as the series progressed. At the beginning of it, I had no views, really. All the theology was someone else's, which I'd soaked up and fed back in, as it were. Towards the end I found my own opinions seeping in.

I'm particularly interested in the interface between Jungian psychology and Christianity. All through the centuries, Christians have been concerned to express their faith in terms of the current philosophy, and now in the twentieth century we have the chance to express it in terms of psychology. I think that's important in communicating with the 'unchurched' masses.

In your Starbridge novels you have made theology interesting to a huge number of people. That's a tremendous accomplishment.

I hope so, because people don't really understand how important theology is. It is basically about wisdom and how to live one's life. If more people understood what it was about, more people would be interested in it.

Your novels seem to achieve something that the church finds difficult. People are willing to explore religion in your novels, but they are less tempted to go inside a church. How come?

I think there are two kinds of evangelism. You can evangelize by preaching to the converted – and that's very important because we all need to be gingered up. But what I'm interested in is this: how do you evangelize people who never go to church and who are just not interested?

You've got to hook their interest. I think you can do this in a story. You can do it by advertising, but that's very controversial. A lot of people in the church think advertising is so, you know, low. I suppose it can be, but every generation has to preach the gospel in their own setting and we're dominated in this generation by the media and by advertising. Just to introduce the idea of God could be quite helpful.

In my novels I treat the church very seriously. I have infinite sympathy for clergymen. I wanted to make my church people attractive and interesting and intelligent and well-educated because, when I was exploring Christianity, one of the most attractive things about it to me was the brilliant and dynamic people who believed in it. So this is what I wanted to get over in the books, and the fact that theology is wisdom, a whole huge discipline like philosophy.

I don't set out to write polemics. But if you are a Christian, what you believe in will come through

You are obviously fond of the Church of England. Does it worry you that the general public seems to have less and less affection for it?

It's an image problem really. When I am asked whether the Church of England is washed up, I always quote Wilberforce: 'The Church of England as it present stands no power on earth can save' – but it's still here. And a hundred years from now it will still be around, but different to what it is today.

Jesus Christ is the same yesterday, today and forever, but the church changes from generation to generation.

Institutions have to change or else they die; but, of course, people find change very difficult.

The clergy you write about are very flawed. They find grace and redemption, but they have to go through some dreadful contortions first.

I'm trying to draw clergymen as real people. We're all very flawed and it's a question of facing up to your faults and seeing them in the light of truth so that you can go on to be a better person.

When I had my great crisis I had to face all the flaws in myself, and I didn't like what I saw at all. By grace you're given the insight to see all your faults and then you repent and are redeemed and resurrected and go on to live a better life. Ideally, that is the Christian pattern of life as well as death.

I have these three main characters [in the Starbridge novels] and the first three books set them up and strip them right down, so that the reader is put in the position of God, knowing more about each character than they know about each other.

There is always some flaw or psychological problem which handicaps them and makes it more difficult for them to serve God, and the story consists of them discovering this and facing up to who they are and what the problem is and trying to emerge as more whole people.

That's why the interface with psychology interests me so much, because Jungian psychology particularly is about integration. Father Christopher Bryant, who did exploration in this area, said that is what the medieval mystics explored: how to line your inner spark, the God within, up with the God without, as it were, to be a whole person. You can serve God so much better if you don't have all this dreadful baggage weighing you down.

Some Christians would say there's too much sex in your novels.

I think a lot of lay people would prefer a clergyman to have no genitals, but I'm not interested in dealing with unrealities. I wanted my clergymen to be real. People say that of course clergymen don't behave like that, but in actual fact they do. Clergymen come up to me and say, 'Thank God someone is finally telling it like it is!'

But in nearly every case – certainly with the three main characters – they got into sexual trouble because they were in some way cut off from God. Sex can be used like drink and drugs, to fill a vacuum or as a narcotic.

My point is that if they do sin sexually, then, when they see themselves in the light of truth, their main concern is to be chaste, to serve God and keep the commandments. So, any graphic descriptions of sex I would say are indications that the central character is in deep trouble. He finally comes to know that and can look back and see it as a symptom of a much more profound maladjustment.

Do you think more fiction writers should be writing about God?

You can only write what you feel you've got to write about. It's a very mysterious process. But novelists in a sense reflect society. Perhaps if society were to change and become more God-aware you would find that the novelists would pick that up.

It would be nice, though, if novelists could write more on moral themes like in Victorian times. A lot of novels today are very nihilistic and very depressing – which again reflects society.

What is the connection between moral standards and Christian orthodoxy?

Christian orthodoxy holds that every person is precious in God's sight. 'Love your neighbour as yourself.' If you believe that, you don't want to hurt people and therefore you get into moral standards. It is all linked.

As far as today goes, it's very dangerous to make hard and fast comments. There has been a decline in the idea

There is a lot of unreality in current discussions of sex. If you think about it, sexual sin hurts people

that this is a Christian country, and people do tend to be governed by the general tenor of society.

The media is controlled by quite a small number of people based in London and we tend to think that everyone is thinking what these people are thinking, and in fact they're not. But if the influential people in London reflect the view that promiscuity or premarital sex is all right, the people in the hinterland are going to think: 'Gosh, everyone thinks this, so perhaps we ought to.'

On the other hand, there seems to me to be a trend in history that nations clamber up the ladder to get rich and then go to pieces. I think we could just be part of a huge trend in which Britain has been very rich and powerful and is now going to pieces. And that always involves a moral decline – the Roman Empire is a classic example. Family values go, homosexuality is allowed to do its own thing, you get a fall in the birth rate and finally economic collapse – and it's like a cycle.

So, the great question now is: Can we get out of this cycle? I don't know whether one actually can.

You've said that 'free love' is dangerous, which is a rather radical view today.

I think there is a lot of unreality in current discussions of sex. If you think about it, sexual sin hurts people. If you propagate the gospel of free love you've also got to figure out how you can justify all the pain and suffering.

I think human beings actually want to make a commitment to people – and, indeed, I would say it was part of a mature personality to be ready to make a commitment to one person.

Promiscuity is a sign that you're not aligned right with God or yourself. I was promiscuous, many years ago now, but finally one morning I woke up and said, 'What am I trying to prove, and to whom? I know exactly what. I'm trying to prove that even though my marriage broke up I can still attract men.' The fact that I could control men boosted my fractured ego.

Obviously, there are great variations in human behaviour. I mustn't fall into the trap of saying everyone's just like me. But a lot of promiscuous people need to take a long, hard look at themselves. I saw a young gay man on the television the other night who was very promiscuous and had unprotected sex all the time, even with people who were HIV positive. I thought to myself: 'That man has a death wish and he doesn't know it.'

The medieval mystics always said: 'Take the journey inwards and know yourself.' A lot of people never pause to ask themselves what they are trying to achieve by their behaviour.

If people who read your novels come to recognize that they are searching for God and are not sure what to do next, what would you say to them?

I often get letters about this. I had a letter asking what books there were for an absolute beginner in Christianity and I wasn't at all sure how to reply. I wrote to about six bishops and – it seems fantastic, I know – they didn't really have many suggestions. One or two old-fashioned ones said, 'Try C. S. Lewis', that sort of thing.

When I started out myself, I just plunged in at the deep end and read everything. Reading is important at such a stage, to acquire the knowledge.

Do you advise people to go to see someone, or suggest how to start a life of prayer?

I have recommended people to the Cowley Fathers here in Westminster, and also to the Marylebone Healing Centre. I wouldn't give advice myself. I'm a novelist, not a spiritual director.

Do you write with your readers in mind?

No. You mustn't think about your readers when you're trying to write. You're prostituting yourself if you write to please someone else. You've got to write what you believe to be true as you see it, or to present a situation in the most truthful light. Otherwise the novel won't ring true.

You have to believe in your own truth. The truth is so enormous that we cannot comprehend it – we're too limited – but we all have our little slivers of truth, our little pin-points, and my aim is to present my sliver. Now, this may not correspond with someone else's, but that's why one can't expect everyone to like what one does. That doesn't mean my work is not true.

And this applies to critics as well, presumably.

Naturally one longs for the critics to drool at one's feet. One's only human. But one shouldn't allow oneself either to be bolstered up so high that one becomes proud or to be so cast down that you're too paralysed by depression to write another word.

Do you feel that God helps you to write?

I think God has liberated me from all the niggling worries: Will the publishers like it? What will the readers think? Will I be on the bestseller list? It's made me more tranquil.

I think my job is simply to write the books and what happens after that is up to God. God will use them in the ways he wants, and if they don't sell as many copies as previously it might not matter, if one reaches just a handful of people. Some people have come up to me and said: 'Such-and-such a book changed my life.' To me, a handful of people like that would be worth the book, no matter who else read it.

And the fact that one's serving God and lined up right with oneself is the way to fulfilment and happiness. A lot of people outside the church have this awful impression that Christianity is all about suffering – you've got to make yourself miserable in order to serve God – whereas the reverse is true. If you're fulfilling yourself and being the person God meant you to be, you will be happy.

Do you find that it is in writing that you are most fully yourself?

Yes. It's a paradox, because when I'm writing I forget myself, so I become more fully myself by becoming unaware of myself. So, in a sense, work is a form of prayer. When I sit down at my writing table, I have the crucifix in front of me and every morning I have eye contact with a victorious Jesus (it's an upbeat Christ, as it were). I offer the work to God for the day and take it from there.

How do you cope now with success?

One's only human. It's nice to be successful because it's affirming in a funny sort of way. At the same time, I would like to feel that if I gave up writing I wouldn't consider my life at an end – there would be more work of some kind to do for God.

Actually, having finished these six books I now have to say to God again: 'What am I required to do?' I think it's time to take stock again. I have a lot of invitations to preach and speak and do this, that and the other; but I don't believe that's my *métier*. I think my *métier* is still to write, but I feel I have to explore all the different options. I'm awaiting instructions. But how do you discern the will of God? That's very difficult.

Success actually is serving God. Real success, spiritual success, is being yourself, being what God created you to be and serving God. Worldly success is very nice and I would be a liar if I said it wasn't, but in the end it's not the be-all and end-all, because it ends. Most writers make the horrible mistake of going on too long; I would like to retire at the top. Lasting success is elsewhere.

How did you come to endow a lectureship in theology and natural science at Cambridge University?

In 1990, I read the books of John Polkinghorne, who is a physicist as well as a priest. I was absolutely riveted. I'm scientifically illiterate (I gave it up at 14), but I saw that this was the future – interdisciplinary studies would open up theology and religion to a lot of people who now are not interested.

I suddenly thought that the twentieth century has been a time when everyone sat in their little disciplines and didn't communicate with each other. In the twenty-first century I see everyone coming out of their little boxes and pooling their ideas. If the world is God's world, then all the disciplines are related and every bit of knowledge is a little sliver of truth – or a big wedge of it.

Then I met John twice by chance (or providence) and I said, 'This is something I would like to do,' and he said: 'Well, we would like to do it very much.' In fact, he had just the week before produced a paper for the university authorities pleading for such a post, and the divinity faculty had been campaigning for it for years.

I wanted to do a chair originally, but that was too expensive – £2 million. I don't have that kind of money, not yet. The lectureship was the second-best thing.

I think it's pathetic when you get these eminent scientists writing eminent books and they make the most appalling metaphysical howlers; and again the reverse is true. John Polkinghorne had just read an enormous book by Jürgen Moltmann about creation which never mentioned physics. In the nineteenth century, the theologians got very much above themselves. In the twenty-first century, they've got to sit down at a table together.

Of course, the dinosaurs in both disciplines are going to fight this sort of thinking, who believe they have the only access to the truth. But they are really a dying breed.

If the world is God's then all the disciplines are related and every bit of knowledge is a little sliver of truth – or a big wedge of it

Is there scope for this kind of interdisciplinary study elsewhere – in theology and literature, for example?

Yes. I think all knowledge comes from God. The difficulty is, there is so much knowledge that no one can be expert in everything. That's why it's all the more important to encourage communication between the disciplines.

BIOGRAPHY

Susan Howatch was born in 1940 and educated at Sutton High School and King's College, London, where she obtained a degree in law.

In 1964, she emigrated to the USA, where she married. She had started writing at the age of 12, and in 1965 her first published novel, a short mystery, appeared. Five more novels on similar lines were followed in 1971 by her first international bestseller, the blockbuster *Penmarric*. Four more sagas culminated in *The Wheel of Fortune* (1984).

In 1975, she separated from her husband and left the USA to live in the Republic of Ireland before returning to England in 1980. By 1983, she was on the road to her conversion to Christianity.

As a result of her conversion, she wrote six novels set in the fictitious cathedral town of Starbridge: *Glittering Images* (1987), *Glamorous Powers* (1988), *Ultimate Prizes* (1989), *Scandalous Risks* (1991), *Mystical Paths* (1992) and *Absolute Truths* (1994). These novels, giving a panoramic view of the Church of England in the mid-twentieth century, explored the Christian cycle of sin, repentance, forgiveness, redemption, resurrection and renewal.

She is now at work completing a trilogy set in modern London and focusing on the ministry of healing. *A Question of Integrity* (titled *The Wonder Worker* in the USA) and *The High Flyer* have already been published.

She endowed the Starbridge Lectureship in Theology and Natural Science at Cambridge University in 1993, and Dr Fraser Watts was appointed to the position on 1 January 1994.

This interview was conducted at Susan Howatch's home in London on 9 December 1993.

At the time of the interview Carolyn Armitage was Editorial Director, Religious Books at Hodder Headline.

NOTES FROM
THE CELESTIAL CITY

Jeremy Begbie talks to the composer
John Tavener

You have often said that you think music has lost its way in the modern world. Can you enlarge on that?

At some point in the Middle Ages – really, the scientific revolution – I see music going downhill because of the gradual emergence of the ego. To give a very simple example: if you look at an icon of the Mother of God holding the infant Christ and you look at a Renaissance picture, it is clear that the second is a humanly executed work of art. And the same with Renaissance music. One can hardly see God for all the trappings.

I feel the Germanic tradition is a man-fabricated system. It's all connected with systems, with the intellect, not allowing any room whatsoever for the Holy Spirit to enter. And I think that is why we've reached the appalling sort of junkyard that the West is in at the moment. The world itself is being burnt to extinction, and we are committing mass genocide with all the relentlessness of a Greek tragedy.

But what about Beethoven, for instance?

Yes, yes, he's humanist – but humanist at its highest, I must say that. If one is talking about hierarchies (which is very unfashionable in this world), I actually think Handel takes humanism even higher. There was a time when I was thinking, 'Western music – I just can't take it at all any more,' but then I heard Handel's *Solomon*, then I listened to *Semele*, and then *Saul* and I thought, 'Here is a composer

> For me, the music of Bach doesn't compare with Byzantine chant. It's not that that is better, or more clever or more beautiful. It's just on a higher level

where the cerebral is not important to him. It just flows out of him.' Of course, a lot of Handel is boring, but when he is at his most spontaneous it just appears to come from nowhere. I am amazed by him.

I compare that with Mozart. I played the first act of *The Marriage of Figaro* on the piano the other day and I thought, 'Yes, it's wonderful, it's perfect, but it's cerebral and contrived. I can still smell the powdered wigs.' In Handel, you can't smell them.

I want to get the balance of this right. I think that in the late works, and particularly in music like the late barcaroles for piano that Beethoven wrote when he was facing death, something divine enters his music. So, I can't be as absolute as the Traditionalists. 'The Spirit lifts us where it wills.'

Where I find Beethoven disappointing is when he him-self starts to come in, as in the *Missa Solemnis* you get his raging at God. Well, who is Beethoven? Who cares about his rage? He is a miserable sinner like all of us.

When you refer to 'Tradition', you mean the Eastern Orthodox tradition out of which virtually all of your music is now written?

That is true. But I think that all great traditions lead to God. That's what I'm trying to say.

How do you define sacred music?

Very difficult. St Paul said, 'It is not I who live but Christ who lives in me.' If you take that a little further and say, 'It is not I who live but Tradition that lives in me,' and you take it even further and say, 'It is not I that compose but the Tradition composes within me,' that's what I mean by 'Tradition'.

St Augustine refers to 'the intellective organ of the heart', and I think that's something that the West has lost. It's nothing to do with the human mind, it's nothing to do with the human heart; it is the area where all revelation takes place – the part of us that we experience when we receive communion, the part of us we experience when we kiss the relics of a saint. It's the part that I experience when I listen to Indian or Sufi music or Byzantine chant.

I do not experience it in any Western music, particularly in the twentieth century. I experience nothing.

Not even in Stravinsky?

Well, Stravinsky's salvation, it seems to me, was the fact that he was Orthodox.

I detest Schoenberg – I consider him and Berg to be the two supreme rotting apples of the twentieth century, because it's rotting humanism.

If you see sacred music in terms of Tradition, where does that leave a composer such as Bach?

I can see that Bach is perhaps the greatest adornment of the Protestant Church, and his music reaches (not by Tradition but by a much more human way) a very high point. But for me it doesn't compare with the music of Byzantine chant. It's not that that is better, not that it's more clever, not that it's more beautiful, none of those things; it's just on a higher level.

In what sense higher?

It has an aspect of compunction, of joy, of sorrow, that hits immediately. You could say that a composer like Mahler hits you like that, but he hits you with a kind of nihilism, whereas the serenity and the vigour of Byzantine chant is almost beyond art. I think we're talking about icons. And you can't put Bach, or any of the Western composers or, in my opinion, any of the Western painters in the same category.

Of course, the music that is most listened to today is neither Beethoven's nor Bach's nor that of the Orthodox Church but pop music. Do you see signs of hope there or do you think it's a dead end?

I don't particularly see signs of hope there; but on the other hand I've often been touched by someone like Randy

Newman, who I think is a believer (not a Christian: I think he's Jewish). He uses a vocabulary of about two words, as against Elliott Carter, who uses a vocabulary of five thousand words, but I would rather have one song by Randy Newman than the entire œuvre of Elliott Carter.

Does the popularity of your own music surprise you?

It surprised me to begin with, but I've had time to reflect on it, and maybe it's because of the way I write, which has nothing to do with traditional classical ways of writing. The music comes from the intellective organ of the heart in me – which is nothing to do with John Tavener the miserable sinner, but with John Tavener who for some reason has come to understand (as far as we can understand, because there is a huge limitation of the human mind) what this intellective organ is. It is so undernourished, it hardly exists; but it is there.

What is the greatest compliment that anyone could pay to your music?

If music or art is truly sacred, it dissects us. Not in an unpleasant way. We do not dissect it; it dissects us.

Do you think that intellectual struggle has a place in composition?

No.

I look at the mathematical schemes in some of your pieces and there is at least an element of calculation. The music doesn't just flow out of you, does it?

Well, it sometimes does. Sometimes does. When it doesn't, the schemes are based on divine and metaphysical formulae.

Can you give me an example of when it has done?

There's a piece I wrote recently, for three very small orchestras, called *Mystagogia*, which lasts well over an hour. All I had was the idea of the Trinity singing as a monad. And I could not stop writing it. I don't know where it was coming from – it's a complete mystery to me. It was dictated writing.

Many other composers have spoken of wrestling with an idea, draft after draft. Does that kind of struggle not have a place in the process?

I would see it as a failing on my part. If I'm going to have to struggle with that sort of angst, I would have nothing to do with the idea. I would scrap it at once.

Have you had periods of creative block?

Yes, but that was before I became Orthodox. I don't want to sound too pat – it isn't as pat as that. This whole concept of the intellective organ of the heart is a much more recent thing that has come gradually, and of course it hasn't come fully. But I think that my attitude now is that if an idea doesn't immediately gel in some way inside me, it has to be rejected.

St Gregory of Nazianzen said that all that is not spontaneous does not exist at all in the eyes of God.

I don't mean that every single long piece that I write I just sit down and do it, but there is an element of not knowing entirely where this thing's come from. The music sometimes appears from nowhere, as if it's being dictated through me, like the late poems of Yeats.

That means really annihilating yourself, annihilating the intellect, annihilating human emotions and also annihilating everything you've been taught, even in religious terms, and just seeing what's there. Maybe there's nothing, but in my case there was: a music started to appear.

> The music sometimes appears from nowhere, as if it's being dictated

And you think that in this way your music is tapping into a deep spiritual yearning in people?

That's the only way I can explain it. The critics don't feel the same way, many of them – well, you know, they need Carter and Boulez because otherwise they have nothing to do. For them, it's like doing crosswords and I don't present anything for them to do.

They can't react to icons, either. Lord Clark, in his book *Civilization*, doesn't even mention them.

There is very little sense in your music of the tension of conflict and resolution that has been part of the stock in trade of the Western tradition – yet some people would say that those same elements are basic to the Christian faith. Do you see it as your duty to point to the resolution only?

That's a pretty big question.

It's one I've been longing to ask you for years. Some people say, 'John Tavener gives us the Resurrection but not the Cross. He gives us a vision of eternity, but not in a way that we can relate to our own struggle.'

I think there's a difference of attitude between the Western and the Eastern Church. In an icon, even when Christ is shown on the cross there is no sign of suffering. As one of the Desert Fathers said: No man is more at peace than when he's on the cross. Our service on Good Friday, for instance, is like a human funeral: it is tender, it is gentle, it has none of the violence or bleakness of the Latin West.

Is that because you are seeing things in the glow of the Resurrection?

Always! 'We glorify your Passion, O Lord. Show us your Resurrection.' Throughout Holy Week, we never stop singing that.

So, there is less of the focus on the Crucifixion that is typical of the Western Church?

Yes. Indeed, a great friend of mine, Cecil Collins – actually, I don't know whether I entirely agree with this – said that the reason for the malaise of the West is the concentration on 'the murdered God', as opposed to the Resurrection.

When I'm writing music, I know God exists. I know that everything Christ said is true

And yet death seems to have been very prominent in your music – much more so than in that of many other contemporary composers.

The very first thing I set to music, when I was 15, was a Donne sonnet, 'Death, be not proud'. Even at that age I must have had a subliminal knowledge of what I was doing. But I now feel closer to that piece that I wrote when I was 15 than to those crazy trips into the avant-garde that I did in the Sixties and Seventies – *The Whale*, the *Celtic Requiem*.

I think that wherever death appeared in those pieces – even in *Ultimos Ritos*, which is concerned with John of the Cross – there is much more violence in that music. Even Donne's sonnets I would say were crypto-Catholic in that setting.

I think I see death now – well, certainly in musical terms – as a friend.

Your music seems to mean a great deal to people who are facing death. Can you account for that?

All I know is that I receive very often letters from people who have been very ill with cancer, or from relatives of people who have died from it, and they speak of the hope that my music has brought.

Often, when people die they seem to leave me some kind of parting gift. *Song for Athene* [which was sung at the memorial service for Diana, Princess of Wales] I wrote in memory of a Greek – half-Greek – girl in her late twenties who was killed in a cycling accident.

I went to her funeral and, as in all Orthodox funerals, the coffin was open and she was dressed in white, and it was the effect of that, I think. When I went home, I sat down at once and started to write.

One could say the piece came to me already born.

What did you make of the mood that seemed to fill the country after the Princess's death?

Either it was hysteria, which would be the more cynical

interpretation, or it reawakened something in the intellective organ of the heart. I mean, why, all of a sudden, did people start lighting candles? It's quite natural for a Greek to do it, but not the English.

I don't think it was pure sentimental love for her. There was something else.

Can music be a friend in the face of death?

Well, definitely. Once, before I had major heart surgery, I was in bed in a very weakened state and I could hardly write but I still went on writing. At the time, I was writing 'The New Jerusalem' (the final section in *The Apocalypse*) and it was a tremendous friend to me.

When I'm writing music, I know God exists. I know that everything Christ said is true. I know. But when I'm not writing music, if you asked me, 'Do you know?', of course I would say I don't: I know nothing.

How do you conceive eternity?

I'm not a theologian.

You are, a theologian through music, very much so.

I like to think of my music as liquid metaphysics.

Can you explain what that means?

Well, I have to have a reason for why I write a certain note, or a certain harmony appears. Therefore, one builds up – from the chant of Byzantium or the Russian Middle Ages, or Indian chant: I don't mind where I take it from – one builds up a language of symbols – there has to be a reason why it's that note and not another – so it becomes a metaphysical idea made incarnate. Does that make sense?

So, the metaphysics is shaping the music?

Entirely. Not the other way round. In fact, I cannot write abstract music, and the concept of art for art's sake repulses me. And that is what we've come to.

Do you think of your pieces as icons?

I can't say that they are. All I can say is that they aspire to be that. I use the word 'icon' (although it's been cheapened, like so many other words in the English language) because that is the way it should be listened to. In no way can an audience listen to a piece by me in a concert hall as they would to – I don't know, Harrison Birtwistle.

My music aspires to be a mirror of heaven, whereas Birtwistle's seems to be a mirror of hell. But there is no intention on my part of proselytizing. In fact, when *The Protecting Veil* was first performed at the Proms I had a letter, from a young girl perhaps, and she asked: did I mean by the title that I was trying to protect unfashionable values like truth and beauty? Well, I mean, that's fine for me.

It didn't bother you that she didn't get the theology?

No, not at all.

Why don't you just compose music for the Orthodox Church, for the liturgy, and forget the concert hall?

Well, basically because they don't want it. I mean, the Greek and the Russian Churches have got a wonderful Tradition of music, and I can't write anything like that. If there were an English Orthodox Church, of course, the situation would be quite different and I would be very happy to be employed as a small-time Bach; but that seems fairly unlikely at the moment.

And my spiritual adviser, Mother Thekla, says, 'You must take what you've learnt from Orthodoxy and take it into the world and into the marketplace.'

Had you ever thought of being ordained?

Well, if I had any thoughts of becoming a monk it was then that Mother Thekla came into my life – both as spiritual mother and as my librettist – and she said, 'I've never heard such rubbish in my life. Forget the idea!' And Metropolitan Anthony was around and he said, 'Absolutely no! You will hear music wherever you are. The abbot may well tell you that you can't write music, and you'll go mad.'

In your music, there seems to be a passion for simplicity – almost as if complexity was something to be avoided, something associated with the Fall.

I think complexity comes from the devil. Tradition says that, anyway.

Is that why at the end of *The Apocalypse* there is this fierce concentration towards a single note?

That is because I was depicting the heavenly Jerusalem. My approach is the *via negativa* always and – what on earth is this heavenly Jerusalem? I don't have any idea. So, it was, I hope, an act of humility on my part, to allow the single note to resonate all round the building.

Being abstruse is a different matter. If you think of that extraordinary last dialogue of Christ, 'I go to the Father' – I'm absolutely certain that it was addressed to his disciples, but I'm not sure that we can possibly understand it. And very often I write in an abstruse way when I am setting words of Christ, because of the esoteric dimension.

I find the Western approach so exoteric, so triumphalist, whereas the Eastern approach is so much more esoteric and non-triumphalist – with the possible exception of Easter night, when we go completely mad.

So, the simplicity you try to achieve in your music is related ultimately to the simplicity of God?

I'd rather use the word 'transparency'. It's that that is important.

Without confusion?

Exactly. Allowing room for the Holy Spirit. Simone Weil (I don't admire her very much now but I used to – well, I still do in a way, but she's very much Sorbonne material) said that art has to have that transparency.

Do you ever feel you were born at the wrong time?

Not really, because – well, maybe I have some kind of vocation, I don't know. Maybe there is something, however small, that it is necessary for me to say, both in words and in music. But I suppose all artists would say that. All artists think, you know, when they are writing it, that the thing they are doing is the most important thing in the world.

What is important is to allow room for the Holy Spirit

Put it another way: I believe nothing happens by accident in life, and therefore there is a reason why I have been incarnated at this particular time. From a purely social point of view, I wish my father was still alive, because I had such a wonderful time with him – we both loved wine and we had wonderful conversations; but no way would I want him back. I would not be a Christian if I did. Does that make sense?

In the Byzantine tradition, the icon painter is a self-negating – indeed, anonymous – figure. How have you come to terms with being a celebrity?

The fact that I have the house in Greece is enormously important: I live in a rural area where there are no tourists and nobody has a clue who I am. That's where I feel happiest. But coming back to Britain doesn't bother me so much – I mean, it's a kind of arrogance in a way to refuse to be photographed, just as you could say it was vanity to want it.

I rather despise those pictures of me that were taken three or four years ago, clutching icons. I think they were in very bad taste. The concept that I was sort of something holier than thou . . . You know, I'm not.

BIOGRAPHY

John Tavener was born in London in 1944 and educated at Highgate School. His first commissioned piece was a *Credo* performed in 1961 at the Presbyterian church where his father was organist.

A year later, he enrolled at the Royal Academy of Music,

where he studied composition under Lennox Berkeley and won several major prizes.

In 1968, he met John Lennon and, soon after, his dramatic cantata *The Whale*, written for the London Sinfonietta for its inaugural concert, was recorded on The Beatles' new Apple label. His reputation was consolidated by (most notably) *In Alium* (1968), *Celtic Requiem* (1969) and *Ultimos Ritos* (1972). His first opera, *Thérèse*, was finished in 1976.

His turn towards Byzantium became evident in *Canticle of the Mother of God* (1976) and *A Gentle Spirit* (1977). After he was received into the Russian Orthodox Church in that year, the tenor of his work became increasingly spiritual. *Ikon of Light* in 1983 was followed by an *Orthodox Vigil Service* (1984), *The Protecting Veil* (1987), the *Akathist of Thanksgiving* (1988), *Resurrection* (1989) and *We Shall See Him As He Is* (1992).

Also in 1992, his second opera, *Mary of Egypt* (for which Mother Thekla wrote the libretto) was premièred at the Aldeburgh Festival and the Virgin Classics recording of *The Protecting Veil* by Steven Isserlis won a Gramophone Award.

His most recent commissions include *Innocence* (1994), written to commemorate the victims of the Second World War; in 1995, *Let's Begin Again*, *Svyati*, *Agraphon*, *Feast of Feasts*, *Prayer to the Holy Trinity* and *Tears of the Angels*; and in 1996 *Vlepondas* and *The Hidden Face*.

In 1997 his popularity was rekindled when his *Song for Athene* was performed at the close of the memorial service in Westminster Abbey for Diana, Princess of Wales. A recording of *Svyati* by Steven Isserlis and the Kiev Chamber Choir was shortlisted for the Mercury Music Prize.

In 1999 Tavener's book *The Music of Silence* was published by Faber and Faber. The year 2000 has seen the premières of two major works at St Paul's Cathedral, *Fall and Resurrection* and *Total Eclipse*. In October 2000 the South Bank Centre presented *Ikons of Light*, a major festival of his music.

John Tavener received a Knighthood in the 2000 New Year's Honours list for 'services to music'.

This interview was conducted at Mr Tavener's home near Hassocks on 6 November 1998.

Jeremy Begbie is Associate Principal of Ridley Hall, Cambridge and Reader in Theology at the University of St Andrews, where he directs the research project 'Theology through the Arts'. He is the author of *Music in God's Purposes* (Handsel Press), *Voicing Creation's Praise: Towards a Theology of the Arts* (T & T Clark) and *Theology, Music and Time* (CUP).

STAND-UP FOR FREEDOM

Nev Pierce and Huw Spanner talk to
the campaigning satirist
Mark Thomas

Satirists come in two kinds. There are those, like Dean Swift, who seem to dislike humanity and delight in exposing its faults, and those who love humanity and are indignant at the gulf between how the world should be and how it actually is. Which kind are you?

I think the capacity to love other people and to care – not just for people who are immediate to you but for people who are a long, long way away, who you will never meet – is fundamental to being a human. It's a fundamental impulse to want to be loved and to want to love, and the two things go together.

It comes across that you feel righteous anger –

Self-righteous, you can say if you like.

But where do you get your moral absolutes from? Are we all born with a common sense of right and wrong?

I think we are born with a sense of being social beings and wishing to co-operate together. If a child falls over in the street, your reaction is to pick it up. You don't have a debate about it to see whether it's profitable to do so. Isn't that an impulse that shows a natural tendency to work for good?

You do not wish to see other people become victims, or

made victims. You do not wish to see other people treated badly. We have an instinct to care.

Do you believe in God?

No. I would like to, I really would, but I have never seen any evidence that would persuade me.

So, how do you account for that sense of morality?

Can I tell you where I last heard that argument? It was from the press officer for the Church of England's investment fund. His argument was: without a Christian belief, how can you have fundamental moral principles?

And I wanted to know from him, 'How come you've fucked up so royally?' You have a look at the companies that the Church of England invests in. Religion has played a role in providing a moral framework, but it's also provided the most untenable excuses for atrocious behaviour.

It's a fair point. All we wondered was, if you don't believe in a Creator, how do you account for our moral instinct, and why does it have any validity?

All I'm saying is, I just wiped out the Creator bit. The urge is still there, the need to love other people. I don't know whether I could explain it in terms of genetics or social conditioning or what. I just know that concern and love for your fellow human beings is there in all of us –

The capacity to love other people and to care is fundamental to being a human

Do you agree that the opposite is also there?

What, hatred and contempt of human beings?

Yes. Or selfishness, or xenophobia ...

I genuinely believe that those bad elements are actually the subject of our upbringing, or of our environment or of predominant thought, where we haven't got the tools to think our way out of it, or whatever.

If you look at people on some of the roughest council estates, you find that the object of their hate and scorn is the people who are just below them, the asylum seekers or gypsies or whatever. It's like, 'Down there, they're scum. I'm better than them. I'm not at the bottom of the pile.'

I think that the main cause of intolerance is greed and the main cause of that is the world you live in, which sees greed as a valuable asset.

So, you think that people's good instincts or habits are innate but people's bad instincts . . .

Are learnt. Are learnt. There is learning involved in how you develop and, if you like, become morally sophisticated; but essentially we're born with the good deck of cards, emotionally and morally.

How many children do you have?

I've got one. One little boy.

It's just that many parents might say that it is self-ishness that is innate and empathy that is learnt.

Oh no! Now you're saying that we're all born sinful, aren't you?

You're basing this on a spiritual analysis, rather than on a genetic analysis or an analysis of society. My position is, I don't know where that innate goodness comes from. I think, if you're completely honest, neither do you. The fact is, it's there.

OK. The usual Christian critique of the traditional left is that it ignores the human propensity to evil as well as good. It tends to say that people are basically good and it's the systems that are wrong –

The propensity for either is really down to how we are brought up, where we live, what we do, what our parents think, what our family thinks, what our society thinks, what our friends think, what opportunities we have, what chances . . . That doesn't apply universally, but by and large I think it holds true.

Anyway, I'm not a leftie.

How do you define yourself?

I define myself as a sort of anarcho-liberal.

The basis of what I would call 'anarchy' is the fact that we work best in groups which co-operate together. We come together and we form our allegiances and alliances and then when it's over, it's over: you go and form alliances with other people. I see anarchy as just an extension of democracy, if you take democracy to mean not the five-yearly little ritual of the cross on the ballot paper but taking control and responsibility for our own lives.

In our day-to-day existence, I'm a liberal in the sense that I think, 'There's no way I'm going to force this on anyone.' I'm not an absolutist. There are problems we have to solve, and you try and get results where you can. You can't take the position of an ideological ghetto and say, 'I am the harbinger of truth and justice. I am the vanguard.' What I don't know is vastly more than what I do know. Do you know what I mean?

Are you an optimist? One reason that apathy sets in is because people think that nothing can be done.

Oh, I think change is always possible, always possible. What is dispiriting is that infantile optimism of the Socialist Workers Party, who say, 'As soon as we organize the first 24-hour strike, bingo! We're on for the revolution.' OK, well, you just carry on.

The number of people who have burnt out from those kinds of organizations because their optimism has been crushed . . .

As you look at Britain in the Noughties, do you think that things are getting better or worse?

It's obvious that we're not living in the anarcho-Zen utopia yet but, you know, there are enormous things that we have achieved in this country. In terms of education, in terms of health, in terms of life expectancy and literacy.

But there are enormous problems still to be overcome.

We have not dealt with the root cause of them. Which is, in my modest opinion, capitalism.

Is there a realistic alternative?
Of course there is. Of course there is.

Apart from violent revolution?
Violence is acceptable only – and only – if you, your family or your community are directly threatened, with no alternative. If you cannot do anything to avoid a confrontation, then and only then is violence acceptable.

You can support other people's decisions. For example, if you look at the Zapatistas in the Chiapas region: their decision to take up arms against the Mexican state was very well thought out, and not made without a lot of soul-searching – and they have continually said that their objectives are peace, justice and democracy. One of the reasons why the Mexican state can't handle it is because they're not after power, they're after basic human rights.

You can support the decision of the Sandinistas to overthrow Somoza. You can support the decision of the ANC to wage war against apartheid. But it doesn't give you by proxy a right to be violent. So, that's the first point.

As for whether there is a challenge to capital, there are two points that I'd make about that: first, I would hope that people with any sense of morality make a decision to take an action not because they can see it as a winnable action but because they see it as a moral obligation. You don't just do something because you think you can win, you do it because you believe it morally right to do so.

The abolition of slavery, when people first mooted that idea, was not exactly popular. People weren't sitting around saying, 'Yeah, that's a vote-winner. We don't have the vote but fuck it, it's a vote-winner.' The point is they did it because they believed it to be morally right, and surely that has got to be the premise for any action we take: do you believe what is happening to be moral or immoral? There

I really believe that there is right and there is wrong and there is very little grey when you really inspect it are grey areas, but they are really, really, really small when it comes to the final analysis. I really believe that there is right and there is wrong and there is very little grey when you really inspect it.

You have remarked in the past that Brecht's play *The Caucasian Chalk Circle* opened your eyes as a young man to the fact that there are two sides to an argument. But what you do is polemical, isn't it?

Ken Loach once did a programme about trade-union bosses selling out and they insisted on the right to reply, and he said, 'I thought I was the right to reply.' I kind of feel like that. I think I am the other side of the argument.

Look at any of the shows in the last series. The first one was on Burma, then there was one on Iraq, one about Nestlé, one on the Export Credit Guarantee Department, one about Aldermaston. In the next lot, there was one on David Shayler, one on Nestlé and GM, one on xenotransplantation, one on the ECGD, one on Jack Straw and the Cambridge Two and then there was a round-up with the Dome. Take up all those examples.

The Government's official line is they will not have sanctions on Burma. Ours was a questioning of that, saying, 'The people here have asked you' – we had tapes of Aung San Suu Kyi saying, 'Get out!' We met with the ambassador: his idea of democracy – well, he doesn't have one, you know.

On Iraq, we were asking why it is that so many people are killed there as a result of sanctions and yet when people sanction-bust, which is against the law, how come they're so reticent to take them to court? Because they're embarrassed.

Nestlé – just getting together all the evidence and saying, 'Look, you've broken your code here, here, here, here. You say this, you do that.'

I could go through every show, and in each one I think we redress an imbalance. So yes, you're right to say to an extent it's a polemic. I challenge you to find any fault with the facts. I'll go toe-to-toe with anyone on the arguments involved. But what we do is represent the argument that is least heard.

How do you account for the discrepancies between what politicians say in opposition and what they actually do in government?

The nearer they get to power, the more compromises they have to make – which is why I don't seek to change that power structure, or replace it. I am not interested in saying, 'I will now begin a benign dictatorship.' I'm not interested.

I refuse to acknowledge that people will not respond, given the facts

Part of the leverage that you've got as a satirist lies in the fact that the people you're attacking claim to be decent and moral even if the things they're doing suggest the opposite. Suppose you came up against a nihilist – like Harry Lime in the Ferris wheel in *The Third Man*. How would you deal with him? Besides being tempted to push him out.

The moral crux of that film is not just about Harry Lime versus the world. It's about Holden's actions as well. And if you were in that box with Harry Lime, knowing that he was supplying adulterated medicines that would kill a vast number of people – it's not about whether you push him out, it's about whether you shop him or not. And the answer is 'Yes. Every time. Every single time.'

It's not about Lime's responsibility; it's about your reactions. You have a moral responsibility to deal with it, and your choice is not 'Do I push him out or do I try and argue with him?' It's 'What do I do to stop this?'

My job isn't to convert them to my ideas or to my values or whatever. It's purely to stop them doing things which cause distress and harm.

You talk about people coming together, forming an alliance to get things done and then moving on. Isn't that a description of government?

No. No. Because government at the moment is essentially

an extension of corporate will. Monetarism is now enshrined within the Bank of England as its predominant doctrine – its actual objective, isn't it? So, you can't say that in any way our democracy is representative of us. Democracy by and large has failed. The Government is predominantly corporate.

So, what is the alternative?

I don't have a blueprint of what people should do. People should take a bit more responsibility and a bit more power into their own hands – whether that is organizing let schemes or putting forward organic food boxes or campaigning against militarism or trying to organize a trade union – or in fact trying to bypass a trade union to form your own grassroots union. Whatever is appropriate.

There is always room to move forward. There is always room to take small steps. People often say to me, 'What's the answer to all this?' I don't know. Find out for yourself. That's the most valid thing.

But a country has to have some sort of foreign policy, for example. You can't leave it up to individuals.

But we haven't got a viable foreign policy as far as I can make out. We've got business as usual. Isn't it absolutely mind-boggling that we have to have an argument over how much it costs to send helicopters to Mozambique? That a country with our wealth and our position in the world squabbles over who's going to pay to pick people out of trees?

Let's take Turkey. We're trying to bring Turkey into the European Union, right? So, what are we doing? We're cutting deals and we're ignoring human-rights violations left, right and centre – ignoring the state of the Kurds, ignoring the fact that people can be arrested on the flimsiest of excuses, ignoring the occupation in Cyprus. Why are we supporting them in that way? Why are Land-Rover building armoured vehicles there by co-licence production?

But you'd like Britain to impose sanctions on Burma and a government could do that. But if you left it to 56 million individuals, how many do you think would say 'Let's do it'? A lot of people just wouldn't care.

I think you're wrong, if the facts were explained to them. I refuse to acknowledge that people will not respond, given the facts. The number of people who are outraged is incredible. I hate to keep going back to Mozambique, but people are very, very touched by the human plight there and they don't think it's right that the Government has wasted time arguing about who's going to pay for the helicopters.

There was no huge groundswell over Rwanda, was there, and the killing went on for weeks and weeks.

I think you're right. People didn't know quite what to do because everyone describes it as tribal. And actually in all wars there is no absolute right and absolute wrong, because no one single community has a clean pair of hands.

But you've also got to remember that people are getting their information from the media, and from government sources. Now, if the Government is promoting a non-interventionist line, that's going to be the predominant line, and the argument then is: Is the Government right or wrong? Rather than: How do we stop this? Do you know what I mean?

So, the news media have an enormous responsibility here, as does the Government. The fact that the conflict went on without intervention does not mean that people don't care. When the positions are explained and people find out about things, they genuinely do care and are willing to take action.

For example, East Timor went on for 25 years. I remember watching the United Nations go in there and just screaming, 'Twenty-five years too late!' at the telly, because that's what it was. But there are people who will have heard of East Timor for the first time because of those news programmes going 'Get in there, get in there!' So, it's information. It's always about information.

Is the Internet going to challenge the status quo as it democratizes people's access to information?

No. But it's interesting. You know, the nice thing is, potentially you've got a library in your living room. Can you imagine having every single book ever written, just a click away? Don't you think that's really exciting? But I think it's just a tool.

There is a revolution in how we communicate – it's not the revolution – but until everyone's got access to the Internet and until it's reasonably cheap to run it, you're still stuck with the same problems. Go down to, I don't know, the Winstanley Estate near Clapham Junction and say to people, 'How many of you believe the revolution is going to start because the Internet is here?'

Do you think that people can operate within the democratic system as it is?

They can operate within it. How effectively, I don't know.

Noam Chomsky has argued that in the United States voters have to choose not between two different parties but between two different wings of the business party. Do we have more of a choice in this country?

Yeah, I think it's people organizing and getting stuff done together. You see it all the time. If you go to a decent church you'll see it: people raising awareness, collecting funds, sorting things out for various causes and campaigns. If you go to decent NGOs you'll see people just getting stuff done.

The people who get things done are at the bottom. As soon as we start to regulate it in big party structures, really we're doomed. But you must see stuff every day that makes you think, 'This is fantastic.' There's a lot more of us out there than people think, who organize and take issues forward and try and create something that's better.

Some years ago, Joanna Lumley was talking about her heroes and she said, 'I just want to see men of kindness and vision and oratory. I long for someone to speak so that our hearts catch fire and we go, "Yes, I'll do that," instead of just thinking, "You tossers."' Is that a sentiment you could echo?

I just wonder how many men of kindness and vision and oratory make the yogurt she advertises.

It depends what you want in a hero. I regard my mate Pete as a hero for the way he works with children. A woman I know called Karen works with sex offenders in rehabilitation units. There's a guy called the Revd Martin Blakebrough, who works at the Kaleidoscope Project, who I think is completely inspirational, I genuinely do.

I think Lindis Percy, who's a Quaker up at Menwith Hill, is inspirational. I think Kathy Kelly, who works with Voices in the Wilderness and takes medicines over to Iraq without export licences and faces imprisonment and ridicule and vitriol and violence, is inspirational. I regard all the people that I see like that as heroes for having the courage and the convictions to go in there and fight for a better way.

Individuals who do the bulk of the work are the people I admire. The leaders and the orators exist on the back of other people's work.

Are there any politicians you genuinely admire?

There are politicians whose actions on certain things I admire but whose general inaction I find abysmal.

Lord Avebury is someone I completely love, because he's there in the House of Lords every time, banging away, doing his stuff. There is no one he's fucking let down. And that's really important. I never thought I'd see the day when I admired someone in the House of Lords, but I admire him immensely.

Aung San Suu Kyi – of course you admire her, of course you regard what she does as heroic. Whether she's that heroic when she's out of that situation, who knows?

There's a lot more of us out there than people think, who organise and take issues forward and try to create something better

No, I think there are plenty of inspirational figures. But please don't expect too much of them.

Have you ever thought, 'It's too much effort. I can't go on being this angry any more'?

I get tired, just like everyone else. But the idea that I'd just go, 'Nah, I've had enough.'

I'm not saying I'm the salvation of anything. I'm just doing my bit. And I'm very happy doing my bit: I'm enjoying it and I think for me it's worthwhile. Three or four years down the line? I don't know.

It goes back to the old gag . . . This mate of mine told me, 'I've been going out with a woman who's an anarchist. I wanted a date and I phoned her up and said, "Are you free?" And she said, "I'm not free until we all are."' And I kind of think, 'Yeah, that's about it.'

BIOGRAPHY

Mark Thomas was born in 1964, the son of a builder and lay-preacher and the grandson of a Blackshirt. He was educated at Christ's Hospital in Horsham, where he was a scholar, and went on to study drama at Bretton Hall College in Wakefield.

He embarked on a career as a stand-up, co-founding the London Comedy Store's show *Cutting Edge* and winning a *Time Out/01 for London* award for his 'distinctive contribution to the art of comedy', as well as a nomination for a Perrier award.

He broke into broadcasting in 1994, as presenter of *Loose Talk* on BBC Radio 1 and as resident stand-up on Channel 4's *Saturday Zoo*.

Two years later, he launched *The Mark Thomas Comedy Product* on Channel 4. The fifth series, now named simply *The Mark Thomas Product*, goes out in 2001.

In 1996, he released a video of his comedy titled *Sex, Filth and Religion*.

This interview was conducted in Mark Thomas's office at Vera Productions in central London on 6 March 2000.

At the time of the interview Nev Pierce was production editor of *Third Way*. He is now Reviews Editor for the film website popcorn.co.uk.

Huw Spanner is publisher of *Third Way* and co-ordinator of Third Way Travel. He contributes occasional Godslots to the *Independent* and 'Thoughts for the Day' to BBC Radio 4.

AN ADVOCATE
FOR ART

Nigel Halliday talks to the
director of the National Gallery
Neil MacGregor

**The National Gallery is marking 2000 with a big
exhibition of paintings of Christ, which you are
deeply involved in. What is the idea behind it?**

There is a huge audience for talks and debates about the
religious subject-matter of paintings. We do a lot of lecturing in front of pictures, and to find that you can easily have
200 people stand for 40 minutes while somebody talks about
the Immaculate Conception is really startling – particularly
in a Protestant country where most people haven't the
slightest idea what it is, never mind why it might be significant. The same goes for the Atonement. And this is a
consistent pattern.

Most of these people would never go to church, they
would never pick up a book on theology; but because it's
in the context of the history of painting which they're interested in, it gives them a way into a cultural tradition which
is also a religious tradition. They might otherwise stumble
across it through music, but the only access that a very large
number of people are ever going to have to this inheritance
is through painting.

That was one observation I found quite startling when I
came to the gallery. The other was that many art critics,
especially in this century, are, quite simply, embarrassed by
this subject matter. It's not ignorance – they know what it
is, they know precisely the textual source; but there's an

embarrassment in talking about it that no other subject matter provokes, and almost an inability to engage with it.

An art historian or critic looking at Bacchus and Ariadne, shall we say, can see that you can't just say 'The story is such-and-such,' but you immediately go on to why that story of abandonment and love and rediscovery is a universal myth and, even if you have never heard of Ariadne and you don't for a second believe in Bacchus' divinity, you can see that it is about something fundamental. There is a great reluctance, or inhibition, or nervousness, to do the same with Christian subject matter. If the text is discussed, it's mentioned as the text and left at that, and why it matters, and why it mattered at the time, is not addressed.

Take Piero's *Baptism*. It has so frequently been discussed in terms of its formal perfection, its geometrical balance, you could almost parody the way people write about it by saying that its main quality is that it leads up to Cézanne. What is not discussed much at all is why the baptism mattered as a subject to Piero and to the people he was painting it for – what the baptism means.

Every city in this country has a great collection of Old Master paintings – which means a great collection of religious paintings; and we decided to try to launch a nationwide debate about what this inheritance can mean, particularly to non-believers.

In your video series *Painting the World* you talk about religious and biblical subjects as if they are on a par with other historical subjects. Is that deliberate?

Yes. I'm not a textual scholar at all, I'm totally illiterate theologically, so I would not be in a position to talk about the textual authenticity of sources; but it seems to me that in terms of cultural history that's not the point. The point is that for the European society in which these pictures were produced, that was the truth. For all except the tiny Jewish population, that was the explanation of the world and of human nature.

The idea that the duty of love is everyday work I find most appealing

Is there an image of Jesus in the exhibition that you particularly respond to?

That's difficult. In terms of the intention of the artist, I think it would certainly be Stanley Spencer's *Christ Carrying the Cross*, 1920. I have to say that I don't find it moves me visually, but it's certainly the idea – that the duty of love is everyday work – that I find the most appealing.

But you're talking about a principle rather than a person. Are there any images that affect you where a personality comes across?

It's not in the exhibition, but it would be Piero's *Baptism*. I think it is the image in Western culture about somebody really acknowledging their own obligations and potentials. It seems to me that what Piero has done is to paint not just the moment when the rest of the world realizes that this is the Son of God but the moment when Jesus himself realizes it, and he is, for the first time, completely aware of all the implications.

How does that come out in the painting?

In that stillness and clarity and complete geometric order. Suddenly, the whole pattern of existence is made clear in the inversion of heaven and earth behind him – because the river is behind, you have the clouds actually below him in a wonderful natural but metaphorical heaven on earth – and the clarity with which he, looking inward, perceives the implications of what he is and how the world is.

I think it's the most powerful image, the one I can engage with most strongly. It's not so much a personality as a perception. It feels as though that's what the artist wanted to address, what the baptism meant to him or what he wanted people to think about it: that here is someone accepting sacrifice, ultimately, but accepting a great deal besides.

Do you have a leaning towards Christianity, or is your interest solely in the historical meaning of pictures?

In personal terms, yes, I was brought up Calvinist.

You have Scottish roots.

Oh yes. Not just roots – quite a lot of soil, too. And because I grew up in that tradition, of course without any imagery or liturgy and with no notion of form, I became fascinated by the other tradition. Long before I studied art history, it seemed to me that pictures offered a way of approaching these questions that – certainly for me – language didn't, and engaged more immediately and left more freedom for meditation. I found it easier to start thinking about the subjects with a picture as a starting-point than with a text.

Is that a failing in Calvinist tradition, the absence of the pictorial?

Yes. The Calvinists were not the only ones, obviously – there's a wider Protestant rejection of the image. One understands, of course, why it happened, but the price of that decision was terribly high – the amputation of a whole imaginative faculty being used religiously, I think.

One could, of course, argue that a lot of religious imagery, rather than assisting meditation, actually distracts it or manipulates it.

Of course, I can see why people felt so strongly that those images were being abused and were getting in the way, and historically I would line up on the side of the Reformers. But Luther would have argued, I think, that the reason you have to focus on the word rather than the image is because the word is certain and clear and unambiguous and the image is necessarily ambiguous and therefore cannot confidently lead you to truth. Well, not many of us now think that language can do that, either: it's a notion of language that is completely unsustainable.

People often dismiss Christianity on the grounds that they can't believe in an old man with a white beard, and yet that is not a biblical image of God ...

That is the problem. One of the things we are looking at in the exhibition and the television series is how we wound up with an agreed notion of the appearance of Christ which is, obviously, a very late cultural construct which, as you say, blocks people who think that's not what he looked like.

The renegotiation of the appearance of Christ is one of the fascinating phenomena of the last couple of generations, as non-Europeans refused, as it were, the image of Christ that was brought to them.

Particularly the Pre-Raphaelite Christ, which used to be so ubiquitous in Sunday school.

Exactly, and because of imperialism that nineteenth-century European Christ is worldwide.

Again, Old Masters very rarely portray Jesus as a helpless baby, which is a crucial point in Christian theology. Even when he is meant to be new-born, he is usually painted as a strapping young lad.

One of the things we're looking at in the exhibition is precisely that question of how you can represent pictorially the humiliation of the Incarnation, which is such a fundamental notion.

What I find interesting is the difference between the literary and visual traditions in expressing paradox. The Hebrew tradition (as I understand it) is that you indicate the ungraspability of God by attributing contradictory attributes to him – the cornerstone and the stumbling block, the lamb and the shepherd – but while paradoxes are very easy to do in language, in terms of painting they don't work. I think one can see a lot of the visual artistic tradition of Western Europe as being about finding ways of making those paradoxes work visually.

Do you think you can detect a difference between pictures of Christ done by artists who believe in what they are painting and those who are just doing it as a commission?

Not really. I would love to be able to say yes, but ultimately the skill in handling the problems of the artistic form is so much the dominant requirement that I think the level of sincerity and engagement is on the whole marginal. It's like writing a poem.

Occasionally, I think, you can point to someone like Rubens . . . We know that he was very devout, and I feel you can see that in the paintings; but if you asked most people, they would find his religious pictures just as artificial as the rest of his work.

Is it really the same with poetry? Surely no one who was not a believer could match the intensity of John Donne or George Herbert?

I agree – but they wouldn't be asked to. The difference is that paintings tend to be commissioned.

Is that a failing of art, that it is possible to fake . . .

I think 'fake' is the wrong word, because the point is the pictorial problem of inducing response in a spectator. The reason, I think, that one can argue so strongly that the Christian experience is central to Western art is because of the insistence, particularly by Francis of Assisi, on the emotional engagement of the believer and the spectator. And how you construct these relations between the object and the spectator to produce a certain kind of response – I don't think that is faking: that seems to me to be the skill the artist possesses.

The exhibition highlights especially three highly controversial twentieth-century paintings: Holman Hunt's *The Light of the World*, the Spencer and

Salvador Dali's *Christ of Saint John of the Cross*. A lot of Christians would look at these and say, 'I don't recognize this as what I believe at all. These artists are just taking the language of my faith and using it to say something entirely different.' Is that a fair criticism?

Absolutely – with the possible exception of Spencer. I'm sure he would still speak very powerfully to almost anybody.

With Graham Sutherland's *Christ in Glory* in the Tetramorphs, these are without question the four images of Christ in twentieth-century Britain that have had by far the biggest public resonance, and they all relate to the tradition, I think, in a very peculiar way – and they relate to contemporary political circumstances in a fascinating way.

I think it is remarkable how the figure of Christ in twentieth-century painting has still been able to carry this extraordinary political charge

Take the Dali. There is this very old Spanish tradition of the crucified Christ embracing the believer. Dali is doing exactly the same. It is the crucified Christ embracing the world, and at one level it's an astonishingly traditional image. We wanted to show that you can't have an artistic creation without an artistic tradition. No artist ever escapes from that.

Also, it raises the interesting question of how evidently political the debate is, because, of course, Dali painted it as a response to Hiroshima. The viewer is put in the position of God the Father looking at this remote, fragile, destructible world, clearly one among many, and between the Creator and the earth is Christ the intermediary – again, very traditional theology.

It's the same with the way Spencer redefines the imagery of the Passion after 1919. Christ carrying the cross in Cookham, he insists, is not a tragic image, because carrying the cross – loving your neighbour – is daily work, like a window-cleaner carrying his ladder or whatever. I think it is very remarkable how, as the religious tide has withdrawn, the figure of Christ in twentieth-century painting has still been able to carry this extraordinary political charge.

You trained originally for the Scottish Bar. What took you from law to the history of art?

Boredom.

Can we go back a bit further? What were the principal influences – the writers, philosophers, thinkers – that shaped you as you grew up?

Oh, Pascal, Pascal. All the doubt, the anguish, the uncertainty – knowing it has to be true because you so want it to be true, and knowing that's not a statable position and so you find other, more respectable ways to articulate it.

The lack of a single position, I think, is what I found so exhilarating about Pascal, and still do: the refusal to take a single position and the acknowledgement that you have to live with the fact that your position will change, that you will find yourself disoriented and destabilized constantly, that disequilibrium is the stable position. I find that terribly affecting and terribly strengthening, that he could actually formulate it like that.

But also what is so thrilling about Pascal is that extraordinary, rational mind recognizing that there are limits to what you can reach through reason – that reason is not the only way to truth and you must insist on non-rational access to it, whether intuitive or whatever. And the image does allow that. It also gives you non-rational access to error, of course; but that is a price I think well worth paying.

Philosophers have been debating what art is for centuries. Do you have a useful definition?

It's about exploring your own experience, isn't it? Exploring your own experience, but understanding its nature and how it relates to everything else, putting you in the scheme of things. Properly addressed and given time, these pictures tell you a lot about what's happening to you and how that relates to what's happening to everybody else. It's about giving shape to your experience. I take a very formalist view in that sense.

Given time, pictures tell you a lot about what's happening to you and how that relates to what's happening to everybody else

Do you think that artists are always thinking in such terms? We who are not artists tend to talk about art in terms of meaning, but they themselves tend to talk about it in practical, formal terms. We might look at a portrait by Rembrandt and admire its profundity, and yet he himself might have said, 'I was just trying to catch the light on his velvet jacket.'

Do you think that some of the 'shape', perhaps, comes about without the artist meaning it to?

I suppose I would start from a literary analogue. Poetry will inevitably have resonance that the poet did not, perhaps, consciously intend, but the intention to shape and to have resonance is indisputable. The higher the quality of the object, I think, the more unpredictable its impact is. But very few artists do not intend to impose a vision or a shape.

Hans Rookmaaker, the Dutch art historian, argued that the Western fine-art tradition comes out of the tradition of Byzantine icons. Is there, then, something intrinsically Christian about our tradition?

Oh yes. Without question.

Obviously, it is the defining mark of Christian culture compared with Islam and Judaism; but also, I think, a religion that wanted art to make the point that the human body was divine and that an individual's suffering could be, had to be, cosmic – that is what has shaped the Western art tradition, isn't it? The relationship between the individual and the cosmic in that sense. And to that extent our visual tradition has been, overwhelmingly, determined by Christianity.

Everyone says that we are moving into a post-Christian society. Do you think that will affect fine art?

I'm not sure it will, because the forces of tradition are so great. The notion of the sanctity of every individual life, I would have thought, is bound to go on shaping what is done, and the language in which we can do it is an inherited Christian one.

But when you look at the work of the Britpack, the unmade beds, the pickled sheep and the pictures taken from inside a washing machine, do you see a continuity with the tradition on display in the National Gallery?

Francisco de Zurbarán's *Bound Lamb* is not a Britpack image, but it is about exactly the same thing as Damien Hirst's *Away from the Flock*, as I understand it. It is not about a sheep, it is about evident innocence about to be destroyed – a message everyone can understand. It is one of those amazing metaphors that works instantly, in language and particularly visually, and you need never have heard of *Agnus Dei*, 'like a lamb to the slaughter', to know exactly what it's about and to respond emotionally and ethically and, indeed, intellectually.

No, I don't really see a disjunction at all.

The money the National Gallery spends in buying a single work of art these days is probably equivalent to the cut in budget of several London boroughs put together. How could you justify the purchase of another Old Master?

First of all, for whatever reason, Old Master paintings are now the most expensive moveable objects in our society. It seems to me a very, very important symbol that those things which our society values most highly and the rich most energetically pursue should be available to every member of society. The Van Goghs that hang here belong to every member of the public and everybody can come and see them on the same terms, and only on the same terms.

But that's not the main point. The main point is that the engagement with a great work of art does, I think, change people, and it changes people in a way that makes it easier for them to cope with their lives. Thousands of people come into this gallery every day, on their way to the office or from it, in a spare half hour, in moments of exhilaration or distress, using it for pleasure, for solace, whatever. The cumulative effect is unquantifiable but I have absolutely no doubt that every day people leave this place – often not having intended to come when they got up – feeling more able to cope.

This is what makes this collection different from any other. There is no other Old Master collection in the world that is used by its public the way this one is. It's one of the astonishing cultural achievements of Britain to make its public museums, particularly this one, part of the daily life of hundreds of thousands of people.

That great art changes you is an old idea. You don't regard it as naive?

Naive? No! I think it's absolutely axiomatic.

Do you see yourself as an opinion former?

There's no doubt that the way you present a collection like this shapes the way that people are going to feel about these objects, and think about them, probably for the rest of their lives. The disposition of works of art of this quality actually says something about them very profound, and a large number of visitors will absorb that without necessarily even realizing. So, to that extent, yes. But not in any conventional sense.

That begs to be deconstructed, doesn't it?

Exactly. When the Sainsbury Wing opened, we took a very radical decision to hang no longer by national school but by date, so that at every period you have Italian hanging beside German beside Netherlandish . . . And that has a very interesting effect on people, because the implicit message is that European culture is very homogeneous in its preoccupations – people are thinking about the same things in different countries and, indeed, the connections are so strong that in a sense it is one culture all the way through.

Increasingly, we are living in an interactive culture. In that sense, an art gallery is very old-fashioned, isn't it? There are no buttons to push.

Yes, but looking is interaction. Someone wanting to come in just to be alone with a great thing – that's what it's about. Looking at a picture is a contemplative experience, and all the lectures, the catalogues, the soundguides, the videos and the CDs are really to equip someone to do that, if they need it. But ultimately it's about you being alone with the painting, isn't it?

In Iris Murdoch's novel *The Bell*, the delightfully scatty heroine comes to the gallery in her emotional ups and downs to get herself sorted out in front of a picture. Murdoch talks of looking very carefully at something you have come to know very well until at last – this wonderful sentence – at last you confront it with a dignity that it has itself conferred. I think that is where the gallery's interactive. It is about that interchange, the real dignity between the viewer and the thing.

> Engagement with a great work of art changes people. I think that is absolutely axiomatic

Our culture is also increasingly image-based rather than verbal, and yet one in which images are divorced from what they refer to, so that crucifixes (for example) become a fashion item without any religious meaning. Is that process reversible? Can we go back?

Yes. That's precisely what this exhibition is about.

But in our culture at large?

Oh, I think absolutely. If you read an image in the way you are talking about, all you can get from it is what you brought to it; but the extraordinary thing about works of high culture is that they offer you also a completely other way of organizing the world and asking the questions. I think people are very quickly aware of that, and very quickly enriched, and I think there's an enormous desire, and a real possibility, to go back to that. I take a very positive view of that.

BIOGRAPHY

Neil MacGregor was born in 1946 and educated at the Glasgow Academy. He read French and German at New College, Oxford, and philosophy at the École Normale Supérieure in Paris for a year, before studying law at Edinburgh University, where he won the Green Prize.

He was called to the Scottish Bar in 1972, but then changed direction to study seventeenth- and nineteenth-century art at the Courtauld Institute of Art in London, where he gained an MA with distinction.

In 1975, he began lecturing in the history of art and architecture at Reading University and also, part-time, at the Courtauld.

From 1981 to 1986, he was editor of *The Burlington Magazine*. In 1987, he was (controversially) appointed director of the National Gallery.

Since then, he has been widely involved in the international art scene, as a member of the supervisory board of the Rijksmuseum in Amsterdam, the board of the Zentralinstitut für Kunstgeschichte in Munich, the Unesco Advisory Group of the Hermitage in St Petersburg and the Visiting Committee of the J. Paul Getty Museum in Malibu. He chaired the UK Conference of National Museum Directors from 1991 to 1997.

He has made a number of television series about paintings – *Painting the World*, *Making Masterpieces* and (in conjunction with the National Gallery Millennium exhibition) *Seeing Salvation*.

He was made an honorary member of the Royal Scottish Academy in 1995, and has received honorary doctorates from the Universities of Edinburgh, Exeter, Glasgow, Leicester, London, Oxford, Reading, Strathclyde and York. He is also an honorary fellow of New College, Oxford and an Honorary Fellow of the British Academy.

This interview was conducted at the National Gallery on 4 February 2000.

Nigel Halliday is a freelance writer and lecturer on modern art. He is the author of *More than a Bookshop: Zwemmer's and Art in the 20th Century* (Philip Wilson), and has edited Hilary Brand and Adrienne Chaplin's *Art and Soul: Signposts for Christians in the Arts* (Solway).

FULLY ENGAGING

Elaine Storkey talks to author
and feminist
Beatrix Campbell

You grew up at a time when the educational system was busy inculcating gender stereotypes about what was proper for girls and what was proper for boys. What were you like in those days?

My father was a kind of Bolshevik, my mother a Communist, and they bequeathed to me that assumption that you intervene in your world

I was inconspicuous, middling, never very clever. My father was a kind of furious British Bolshevik, a bibliophile, self-educated; my mother was Dutch and a Christian, from a culture of good citizenship, who became a Communist in her fifties. Our family would have been typical of a certain shard of the respectable working class: upward-striving, literate . . .

It was a family that didn't assume you were going to be what they were. But they were very active and committed politically, and that assumption that you would intervene and engage in your world was bequeathed to me, and that culture of working-class respectability that created the welfare state and was behind the 1944 Education Act (two things of which I would be a beneficiary).

Can you speak Dutch?

No. We grew up in a small border town that would have had little or no experience of black people, Jews – even Catholics. So, my mother felt ashamed of her accent and felt it was very important that none of us spoke Dutch, because we would somehow be demeaned by a connection to an immigrant. She was typical of people who felt that in order to survive in Britain they had to conceal any evidence of their origins.

Were you rebellious at school?

I only discovered in adult life, through the women's liberation movement, the stuff to do with gender. At school, we may have mutinied or revolted, but we would have been stuck within certain typical templates – you know, you would either be into sex and smoking, or . . . I suppose that for many girls being clever and getting to grammar school was a way of transcending both gender and class.

The gender stereotyping was to me less palpable than the class defeat of the 11-Plus. The cruelty of the education system for someone like me and, I imagine – well, I know – many like me was disastrous. We forget how absolutely devastating it was for the 75 per cent of children who failed the 11-Plus.

The very idea that there is anything remotely valuable in making the majority of the population live with an experience of failure escapes me. I suppose certain kinds of politics need those sorts of defeats.

What opened your eyes to sexual politics?

It was precisely the women's liberation movement. I don't think I thought about sexism until then. That isn't to say that it wasn't present and palpable in a person's life, but I didn't have a way of thinking about it. You see, socialist politics don't help women think about gender (and they don't help men). They are as sexist as any other kind of politics – or worse, I often think, because socialism promises equality but speaks with forked tongue.

I can remember the first time I was in a room as an adult that only had women in it, and it felt ecstatic, thrilling, dangerous, and very odd. But I resisted the women's liberation movement initially: I wrote a contemptuous article which argued that it was just a movement of middle-class women who were pissed off that they didn't have servants.

The man I was married to at the time – who was a Scots-man and a former engineer, and then boxing correspondent of the *Daily Worker*, would you believe – thought the movement was great. And my mother thought I'd lost my marbles, and became an active feminist herself. So, I changed my mind.

Was that a gradual process?

I think it was instant. You see, this was happening in the late Sixties and early Seventies, and I didn't wake up until the Seventies. Till then, I had been in a kind of emotional slum-ber. I think that was true for a lot of women: the Seventies was the time when we came alive.

What the women's liberation movement then did, of course, was to allow the women of our generation to trawl our own feelings and thoughts afresh. Where did you start? I mean, everything was a challenge. And it didn't stop. In a sense, the more you knew, the more you knew; the more you changed, the more you changed. I think our generation in that respect are astonishing.

I understand that the Sixties was a smashing decade and one that was full of tumult and wonder, and it was a period associated with the great social movements for civil rights (to which we all owe a debt that can never be measured, I believe). But it also maximized the exploitation of women. Young women were both intensely exploited and under the illusion that they weren't, that exploitation was equiva-lent to emancipation, particularly at the level of sex. And out of that contradiction comes the women's liberation movement.

And that history is very important, because the challenges that the social movements of the Sixties and Seventies represent confront many of the old values that the new conservatisms – including New Labour – are revisiting and rehabilitating. New Labour is a very good example of the rehabilitation of old misogyny – in a more covert form, no doubt.

Germaine Greer's book, *The Whole Woman*, suggests that in 30 years women have progressed a long way and then gone backwards. For her, the picture now is extremely gloomy. Is it for you?

It's not gloomy in this sense, that globally patriarchy as a way of running the world has lost its legitimacy. It doesn't mean it's lost power and it doesn't mean it will give in, and it's clear that some of the great combustions in the world are sponsored by patriarchy.

There are many fundamentalisms, both secular and religious, ploughing the world up as we speak – New Labour has its own, that it wears with pride – and most of them will defend the patriarchal principle. But there is no question that they *have* to defend it. The women's movement has changed the terms of politics. We all know what we mean by 'misogyny'; we all know what we mean by 'male chauvinist pig'. We all know that the gladiatorial stuff coming out of the White House and Westminster at the moment is laddishness with a new lease of life. We have a way of reading state-sponsored violence through the filter of feminism that we didn't before.

There are all sorts of things that have changed dramatically. Permanently or not, we don't know; but they are part of an argument that society is having with itself. So, I don't agree with Germaine, even if I understand the pessimism of many feminists.

Recently, you have been very critical of the Prince of Wales and the Windsors. What set you onto them?

I wasn't remotely interested in the Royals, knew nothing about kings and queens, nothing. But when Andrew Morton's book on Diana appeared,[1] it became very clear to me that this man had all the power and all the resources to do something different with his horrible history – certainly, to live with women in a different way – and he decided not to. And what he did instead was premeditated and purposeful, and he did it in the service of his own ambition.

And it felt terribly challenging, because a lot of progressive people had been quite sympathetic to Prince Charles – he had been the one who worried about architecture and vegetarianism and standards: he was a worried man. Indeed, I remember *Marxism Today* ran a cover with him on it and the headline was 'Her Majesty's Opposition'. So, in the becalmed late Eighties, the revelations about the way he treated this young woman were searing and very serious.

I started to think that the left didn't have a way of thinking about royalty: it either buckled to its knees or it thought, 'Oh, it doesn't matter.' But the Royal Family is actually part of the cement of an extraordinarily abusive and hierarchical political and class structure. It was obviously a problem that we didn't have a republican left. In fact, the Labour Party, in particular, has been the Royal Family's friend right through the twentieth century, and secured its survival. Republicans were jeered at and regarded as potty.

And is the Church of England complicit in all this?

Utterly complicit. Its hierarchy knew that the Prince's marriage was a gross deception of a young woman and participated in it, sagely if worriedly. Probably more than any other institution, the Church had access to the secrets of the House of Windsor.

Do you think Robert Runcie knew that the Prince was having it off with someone else? I'm not sure he was so in touch. I know that he thought she wasn't treated very well, and that seems to have disturbed him.

He probably knew that it was ridiculous that a man in his thirties marries a girl of, what, 18, 19, who has been nowhere and done nothing.

Have you always felt critical of the church?

Spooked by it, more than anything. Didn't like Sunday school. Never, ever understood the notion of a God, never

I've never understood the notion of a God. I've never had a single feeling that felt remotely religious. I've just never got it been attracted to it. Always felt vaguely and idly alienated from it. And the religious experiences some people have – which do have to be taken seriously – I've never had. I've never had a single feeling that felt remotely religious. I've just never got it.

Though your mother had a Christian commitment...

If you ask her, as I have done, 'Are you a Christian? Do you believe in God?' she'll say, 'It depends who I'm talking to.' She comes from the sort of non-conformist Protestant culture that is a very significant part of popular culture in Holland. But in the Fifties, I suppose, it kind of faded.

But her politics had similar priorities, and the kind of things she got involved with after her children had grown up I suppose would have signified that merger of her Christian faith and her Communism. She worked as a nurse, she became a very active peace person. There would have been a lot of people who, like her, had values that were looking for a home. And for some it was in organized religion and for some it was in organized politics.

Let's talk about your book *Wigan Pier Revisited*. Why did you want to go back there?

It was an inspired commission by Virago: with 1984 coming up, it felt like a resonant moment. I said yes instantly, although I was never interested in George Orwell – a bit like religion, I just never got it. I didn't like the original *Wigan Pier*.[2] In fact, I think Orwell's horrible, really.

Why?

I think he's mean-minded. He's got a snob's combination of class contempt and class sentimentality, and sees the working class as a class without brain or culture but with, now and again, a touch of nobility. But if you're of the working class, first of all you are of the majority class. And you're not sentimental about it: you're in an argument with it. And I was of, and feel that I am still in, the majority class – like most of the British population, who for some reason, despite the best efforts of Thatcherism, still think they're working class.

I don't hold with a view of the working class as a kind of incipient class, a class that is yet to be made. But I feel that it's a tragic class in one sense, and its tragedy is probably patriarchy. What was given to it as a gift was the mission of political change, and that mission has been endlessly undermined by men.

I don't mean that men are beasts, but from the middle of the nineteenth century it became clear that the women of the working class had been defeated and that its politics had been shaped by a gender that was prepared to exercise its own will at the expense of its own mothers and sisters, its own kin. And so working-class politics have tended to be conservative, sectional, sectarian, myopic – at the same time as promising emancipation, equality and empowerment.

So, *Wigan Pier* became a journey across territory that was then unfamiliar, because Britain in the early Eighties didn't quite know who it was, and the presence of a kind of permanent pauperized population was something that seemed completely new.

And then there was the question: What has common-sense social democracy got to say about this? Because that, in a sense, is what Orwell's bequest is to British politics. And, apart from the odd dose of moral outrage, it's got nothing to say. And that is partly because Orwell doesn't see ingenuity in the working class, nor does he see a conflict within it.

I'm also intrigued by *The Iron Ladies*, which is a genuine attempt to understand some women with whom you have almost nothing in common.

Most of these books, I have to say, were somebody else's idea. But, after Virago suggested it, I got completely riveted. It wasn't worth doing if it was going to be another scornful dismissal of those daft Tory women with hats. I wanted to

As a lesbian, people think I must hate men. But I just don't fancy them. And, like a lot of women, I don't like the way they go about their business know why Conservatism makes sense to these women. In what ways does it help them be in the world? And explain the world?

And without that approach the Tories wouldn't have co-operated: they would have thought, 'This is just another horrible Marxist who wants to rubbish us.' But when I went to Central Office, Emma Nicholson (who was then a vice-chair*man* of the party) looked me in the eye, asked me what I wanted and, when I explained, agreed to be completely co-operative. And she was. And the individual women, in Birmingham, the Borders and London, were terrific.

It's a weird thing to say, but nobody had ever taken them seriously – not even their own party. So, someone actually asking them what they thought about this, that and the other . . . Like anybody else, they felt grateful for somebody else's curiosity.

I get the feeling you have more sympathy with them than with the women of New Labour.

No, but there are less contradictions in their history, certainly, in that their party, which has been astonishingly successful, was never an egalitarian party, and so, I think, they never experienced that terrible sense of betrayal. They attached themselves to a party that was about power, and they put themselves close to power; but they didn't expect the party to do anything for them, other than speak for them.

I learnt a lot from them, actually, about politics and about how people connect with it. Anyone who organizes a focus group would be well advised to learn from them, because they take it all with a pinch of salt. Their expectations of politics and parties are minimal. And so they nest like cuckoos wherever they can that is going to give them a bit of space, a bit of respect, a bit of pleasure and a little bit of power.

And they look to the left and what they see is a macho men's movement that isn't democratic and doesn't deliver what it says it believes in: an egalitarian, open, transparent, accountable politics. And they're not wrong.

Do you think Labour could ever have delivered it?
Yes, absolutely.

In recent times?
I think it had a chance to connect to the great new social movements of the Sixties and Seventies, and the GLC tried to do that. Now, I wouldn't want to go to the stake for the GLC, but what it was beginning to do in the first half of the Eighties, I suppose, was to look at who its citizens were and whether it represented them and was in a conversation with them. And that was a very important moment of modernization. Also in the Eighties feminism began to be felt in the Labour Party. And so Labour's unrepresentativeness was being challenged, and in a sense repaired.

But I suppose that was a challenge to the whole history of the party, and because it's an institutionalized party, not a party of movement or a party of culture, not a party that is very good at actually just being in society, it responded to these pressures in a statist way, and it didn't learn from the subtleties of ordinary, mortal survival strategies.

A lot of writing is suggesting that it is now acceptable politically to be gay, but only if you are a man. For lesbians, nothing's changed. Is that how you see it?
Well, I think everything is always harder for women. Everything. So, your sexuality is under scrutiny anyway, and there'll always be some bloke who thinks he's going to be the one who is going to redeem you from this awful, blighted but exotic condition ...

And for lesbians there's a political price to pay, which is that your feminism is always misread as, 'Well, you just hate men, don't you?' I know from my experience that people will think I'm absolutely ferocious and that I must hate men. They don't think about the fact that I've been married and that for 30 years till he died I had a very important relationship with the man I was married to – we organized an excellent divorce and remained excellent friends.

I live with boys, and I have men in my family, for God's sake. You'd think that you lived in this kind of purdah if you're a lesbian – that there are no men, and anyway you hate them. And it's not true: you just don't fancy them. And, like a lot of women, you don't like the way they go about their business.

Christianity has a strong conception of sexual ethics. How do you frame your own?

My starting point, I suppose, would be feminism, and what it's interested in is power and powerlessness and pain. And so it has a different filter through which it reads a sexual life. So, for instance, the moral re-armers of New Labour are no surprise, because they are doing what traditional orthodoxies have always done, which is defend traditional power.

And why do they all close ranks?

I suppose they have to, don't they? Because they're men. If women's critique, and women's disappointment, and women's values, are allowed to enter their domain, they're in big trouble. It means that they've got to have democratic relationships, and they don't know how to do that. None of these men do. So, when we are lectured by the married Christian men's movement – sorry – by people like Jack Straw, Paul Boateng and Blair, about crime and feral children and how disgraceful council estates are and the collapse of civilization as we know it and 'This will be cracked by getting married, mate,' you think, 'What planet are you on? The one thing you might do that would really make a difference is to talk about how men need to wise up.' They need help to work out a democratic deal with women and children. And they could do something very simple and very longed-for by women, which is just co-operate.

I'm not saying that women are angels; we're as horrible as the next person. But that is the great issue of our time, and these blokes, modernizers to a man, can't bring themselves to say it. So, they waffle on about marriage, without ever asking themselves: Why would millions of women embrace poverty and loneliness rather than be with some pillock?

And what's your answer?

Because staying with a man who gives you pain and disappointment and grief is worse. It's a desert. A desert. We know from what women have told us that it is just an awful place to be, and sometimes a deadly dangerous place.

And to not take that seriously is a terrible political crime, because these men could do something very useful: they could help men to sort out a new relationship with women. What they underestimate is the extraordinary lengths women will go to to make that possible. They absolutely underestimate how much goodwill we bring to that project. And that includes people like me, whose desire doesn't lie with men, you know, but with women, but who want our collective relationship with men to work.

And they don't get that. Something is more important to them, and that is defending themselves, and their power, and their history and their secrets.

In the church at the moment there is a movement, among both men and women, to address the future of our relationships, both sexual and otherwise.

I believe you. I think that, paradoxically, the church is a defender of some of these terrible traditions but also a space in which people have clearly been able to engage in a searching debate about what masculinity is, what femininity is, what's the deal between men and women, who should have power, what's your relationship to God, who is God anyway.

Very, very interesting. I mean, it's not my culture, but I think it's clearly a very productive place for people to have that conversation, and it has clearly been a very productive place also for lots of people to think about their sexual orientation and their sexual responsibilities and the whole shebang. Excellent!

And it's probably a better place than politics is at the moment for having that conversation.

Certainly, a different view of God is emerging in the church that gives people more space to relate to one another. Instead of thinking of God as male and rather tyrannical, we see Someone who calls people into better kinds of relationships that are more about empowerment, forgiveness and mutual vulnerability.

It's interesting you say this, because I am aware there are people within the church who are having a really strong think about all of that, and about how to redeem religion. I've met some incredible Vatican II nuns who are just lovely women, and are clearly very intrepid, and very creative, Christians.

So, without being close to it or knowing anything about it, I absolutely can recognize what you're saying. I could see that the church would be a space for very interesting thinking.

What are your own aspirations for the future?

To work for the day when women will know greater freedom in their lives, and when many of their hardships will be in the past. And to be happy.

Are you happy now?

I'm very well loved. I don't know that I love well, but I try to. And I am fed and sheltered, and curious. And very privileged.

Notes
1 *Diana, Her True Story* (O'Mara Books, 1992).
2 *The Road to Wigan Pier* (Victor Gollancz, 1937).

When we are lectured by married Christian men about the collapse of civilization as we know it, you think 'What planet are you on?'

BIOGRAPHY

Beatrix Campbell was born in 1947 and educated at Harraby Secondary and Carlisle County High Schools.

From 1967 to 1976, she worked for the *Morning Star* as a sub-editor and reporter. In 1971, she co-founded the women's liberation journal *Red Rag*, and (in 1980) *Politics and Power*.

After two years studying planning at the Architectural Association, she joined *Time Out* in 1978, before leaving after a protracted dispute over equal pay (along with most of the magazine's staff) to launch the rival *City Limits* in 1981. She went freelance in 1988.

Her journalism has appeared variously in *The Times*, the *Guardian*, the *Observer*, *New Statesman*, *Marxism Today*, *Scotland on Sunday*, the *Scotsman*, the *Yorkshire Post*, the *Express*, the *Sunday Mirror*, the *Pink Paper* and *Diva*.

She has given lectures and seminars in universities in Britain, Ireland, the United States, Canada and Australia, on subjects ranging from sexual politics to policing.

She has made several documentaries for television, including, in the late Eighties, *I Shot My Husband and No One Asked Me Why*, an edition of *Diverse Reports* on Sinn Féin and one of *Dispatches*, on the Nottingham child-abuse controversy, which won her a First Time Producers Award from the Independent Television Producers in 1990.

She has also contributed to BBC1's *Question Time* and BBC2's *Newsnight* and *After Dark*, and to BBC Radio 4's *Any Questions*, *The Moral Maze* and *Woman's Hour*. She broadcasts weekly to Australia.

She is the author of *Sweet Freedom* (1982) with Anna Coote, *Wigan Pier Revisited* (1984), which won the Chelten-ham Literature Festival Prize, *The Iron Ladies* (1987), which won the Fawcett Society Prize, *Unofficial Secrets* (1988) and *Goliath* (1993).

She was named campaigning journalist of the year by the 300 Group in 1989.

She has been awarded honorary doctorates by the Open University and Oxford Brookes and Salford Universities, and in 1997 was elected to a Simon Fellowship at Manchester University.

She was married in 1968, and divorced ten years later. She came out in 1973.

This interview was conducted in London on 19 April 1999, en route from Westminster Central Hall to King's Cross and Newcastle-upon-Tyne.

Elaine Storkey supervises PhD students in theology at King's College, London. From 1991 to 1998, she was executive director of the Institute for Contemporary Christianity. Previously, she taught philosophy and sociology variously at Stirling and Oxford and for the Open University. Her many books include *Contributions to Christian Feminism* (Christian Impact) and *The Search for Intimacy* (Hodder & Stoughton), and the classic *What's Right with Feminism*, which she is at present revising for SPCK. *Conversations on Christian Feminism* with Margaret Hebblethwaite (Harper-Collins), and *Created or Constructed? The Great Gender Debate* (Paternoster Press) were both published in 1999.

SOUND OF HEART

Jolyon Mitchell talks to the composer
James MacMillan

Why do you think we are seeing such a flourishing of 'spiritual' composers such as John Tavener, Henryk Górecki and Arvo Pärt?

It's hard to say. The music of those three composers is very beautiful and I think people would recognize that whether it was spiritual or not. But I think one can also say that, especially in our time, there is a hunger for something to fill the spiritual void, and some of this music at least gives people a kind of folk memory of what spiritual sustenance was about.

Music and spirituality are very closely entwined anyway – you could say that music is the most spiritual of the arts. More than other arts, I think, it seems to get down into the crevices of the human-divine experience. You can't really express why it moves you so much, but it does. We talk of music speaking to us as if it's a language, and we hear it speaking fluently and profoundly to us in our secret selves; but we cannot really put into words what it's saying.

Also, music is a kind of analogue for the direct and effective communication of grace. Maybe that's the linguistic aspect of it: it seems to come directly from a divine source. People talk, perhaps haltingly, of music having that kind of impact.

> **Music is the most spiritual of the arts. More than other arts, it seems to get down into the crevices of the human-divine experience**

What exactly do you mean by 'the crevices'?

I think there are unexplored depths to the human spirit which are sometimes reached through divine inspiration. We have the facility to discover more about ourselves and about the nature of God through traditional spirituality, but that's a route that many in the West now have cut off for themselves. I think that music seems to remind us of something that was perhaps more of a common spiritual experience, that does seem to get to those depths in the human soul. It has the power to look into the abyss as well as to the transcendent heights, and it can spark the most severe and conflicting extremes of feeling.

It's in these dark and dingy places, where the soul is probably closest to its source, its relationship with God, that music can spark life that has lain dormant for a long time.

Why are you so attracted to ancient church music?

I think the plainchants and so on that I am always using in my music root me in something very deep, culturally and spiritually. I'm plugging into a rich seam, because Gregorian chant is, melodically, probably the most perfect music. But it's the liturgy and the theology that draw me to it in the first place. With my music there is always a pre-musical reason for wanting to compose.

That's a rather odd position to be in, because one could argue that music is the most abstract of the arts – its nature is sound, and the organization of sound. And there is a rightful pride among composers that it seems to be complete in itself – that at a fundamental level it speaks fully in itself. But that has sometimes led to excesses in certain understandings of music, and in the twentieth century to a situation where music as a form has become divorced from the idea of communication, outside a small élite of the initiated. And that is the danger, that music has this facility to retreat into itself.

The bottom line for me in all my musical experiences and enthusiasms has been a recognition that it has a transformative power and – maybe it is something to do with the analogy of grace – that it does change us. Music-lovers speak, almost to a man and woman, of the power of music changing their lives. People have had profound experiences which have transformed them, against their wishes or even unexpectedly: they have not taken a conscious decision to change.

I think there's a very strong analogy between listening to music and listening to God through prayer. In both cases, being prepared to put time aside to listen properly is something that initially, deep down, we all have a reluctance to do. We furiously resist the instinct to pray because we know it means sacrificing some of our precious time to something that is intangible, and we have more important things to do.

But at the root of both there is a fear, almost a terror, of being changed. I think prayer does change us. Our convictions, our activities, our perspectives on our fellow humans, the nature of life, the nature of God, can be radically altered through giving up time to prayer. And it is the same with music. I think our perspectives are fundamentally changed through the power of music. There is an analogy there, and I think it is because they are from the same source: we are talking about the same thing.

Do you find that music helps you to pray?

I don't listen to music to pray. I would say that the act of composition is a kind of prayer, because it means being open to that source. It involves a lot of silence and solitude, and an act of hearing. It means setting aside time in a terrifying way that brings about transformation – the transformation of one's abstract ideas into music.

Does prayer have an effect on your composition?

I believe that music is inspired: it has to do with more than just one's own conscious choices. It wouldn't happen without those conscious choices, but it is inspired by, I believe, the Holy Spirit. The analogy that I like to make – perhaps because I'm a Catholic – is of the Virgin Mary being open to the transforming power of the Holy Spirit at the Annunciation.

Mary is a very powerful figure for me. Not just because of my upbringing, but in the gradual realization as an artist that that silent openness is very similar to the way that artists open themselves up to the power of the Holy Spirit in wishing themselves to be vessels of something.

Not mindless, empty vessels, where something passes through and nothing is affected. It is through the interaction of whatever it is with one's own corporeal realities, one's own senses, one's own intellect, one's own will (because Mary's free will was a crucial factor in the Incarnation) that new art comes about. It is not just one or the other: it's the interaction of both. And so I regard artists as paradigmatically female, in being open to the power of God.

I think that with every new piece that is conceived and gestates and comes to fruition in the mind of the composer, a little incarnation happens.

Is the process of composition, then, an act of discovery or an act of creation?

I think it's both. I know that I discover something unknown about myself with every piece that I write, and that is part of the terror at seeing the blank page. It's not just 'Have I run out of ideas?' It's 'What on earth is going to come forth next?'

What was the thinking behind your fusion of ancient liturgy with recent poems about the 'disappeared'?

I've done this twice. *Busquéda* set the poems of the mothers of the disappeared from Argentina. When I found those poems, I was struck by their power, the emotional impact. They are not sophisticated literature, but the fact that these women were mothers of the disappeared provoked something angry, fierce, loving, hopeful, grief-stricken from them.

And I was struck by the simple and traditional faith lying behind the poems. Even some of the language they used reminded me of liturgical texts like the *Kyrie*, the *Gloria* (because some are deeply celebratory poems of the lives of their lost loved ones), the *Credo* – there is a sense that, in spite of all that has happened to them, they are relying on a deep well of ordinary, simple faith.

I think what I wanted to do was to bring together the timeless and the contemporary, the secular and the sacred – perhaps mutually exclusive concepts in many ways, but I've always been curious to find parallels and connections between them. I'm intrigued by the dialogue between the message of the Gospels and the secular left (I joined the Young Communist League when I was 14). I'm not a Communist any more, but I've always been intrigued by the engagement between politics and religion, the conflict and the contradiction, but also the synthesis of ideas that sometimes comes about.

Busquéda and *Cantos Sagrados* were my first attempts to make powerful and perceptible connections between the musical and the extra-musical, the religious and the political. I describe those two pieces as liberation-theology pieces.

Is it possible to explore such ideas in more abstract music, which does not have text and isn't staged?

It's easier in work where music can engage with the other, more representational arts. But I think there's an ethical dimension that informs a lot of my other music. *The Confession of Isobel Gowdie* was inspired by a story of a woman, a kind of archetypal figure from history, actually, who seemed to represent the outsider in our midst and the way that outsider always seems to succumb to our hatred.

So, there is an ethical dimension even in the instinct to write abstract music. This is the controversial point. It seems to be regarded as a step too far by many musicians. It's something to do with the fact that they like to think of themselves as high priests of a craft, and if it is suddenly opened to the four winds and the ends of the earth, where anybody can get access to an understanding of what it's about, and everybody's pitching in – psychologists and theologians and politicians – they don't like it. That's why I call their restrictive and rather puritanical attitudes to music a selective anti-intellectualism.

It is often said that Tavener's music is a celebration of the risen Christ. Your music seems to be preoccupied much more with the crucified Christ. You seem to be drawn again and again to the Passion.

You're right, I am drawn by the sacrificial aspect of the great Christian narrative, and I seem to be going round and round in circles round the same three days in history. The fact is that if history had to be changed – if *we* had to be changed – then God had to interact with us in a severe way. You can't have the Resurrection without the Crucifixion.

There is a sense of the transcendent in a number of these composers which is beautiful, but there is a deliberate avoidance of conflict – aesthetically and even technically, in the work of Tavener. He has turned his back on that whole aspect of the Western canon. The symphonic form and the sonata form are all about pitting against each other widely contrasting materials, and I'm attracted to that. I'm attracted to it in Beethoven and Mozart, in Tippett, in a lot of modernist music. My character needs that sense of conflict. In purely musical terms, I need to create drama, to tell a story: and the best stories are ones that have resolutions of conflict, not just resolution.

I think that a lot of so-called spiritual music can be a monodimensional experience of transcendence without the sense of sacrifice. My symphony *Vigil* is an Easter piece, but a lot of it is very dark (though it does get to the light). My opera *Visitatio Sepulchri* is quite violent.

Music is inspired, I believe, by the Holy Spirit. With every new piece, a little incarnation happens

Do you think you will ever tire of circling 'the same three days'?

I don't think so. It's too rich a seam, first of all.

Michael [Symmons] Roberts has used the term 'the deep mathematics of creation': music seems to be a means of calculating not just human nature but the very face of God, and one way of doing that is to circle round the very moments when he made his deepest interaction with human history.

So, I know I'm onto something. That's why I'm drawn back obsessively: I can't help it. I know that the answer is here. It's like, open these doors and you'll find the face of God behind them.

Is there a tension in trying to express that aesthetically when what you see when you open the door is something ugly – an execution?

I've got a feeling that the face of God would be an awesome sight if we could ever see it with human eyes. There is something frightening about the presence of God. It's not an evil presence, of course, but it's something that should inspire fear; and it seems entirely appropriate, then, that one way – *the* way – of finding access to that awe and fear is to experience God through the death and resurrection of his Son.

Perhaps the reason I have also drawn on quite frightening instances of human activity in our own time is that with Isobel Gowdie or the mothers of the disappeared you are encountering the crucifixion narrative afresh, in the lives of ordinary people. So, even though there is a political story here, it is like a mirror image or a resonance of the archetypal story.

And to ignore that, and not to face up to the abyss which can sometimes be human experience, is a flight from reality and from, I think, the true nature of God. Spirituality is not just some sort of easy-won feelgood factor. You find it in the here and now, in the grit and the mire of human life, and you raise the possibilities of compassion in those encounters.

Wanting to bring an end to suffering, to bring a redemption through crucifixion is, I think, part of the Christian artist's instincts

When you see on your television the refugees streaming out of Kosovo, does that inspire you, or are those glimpses of suffering blocks to your composition?

It makes me want to compose. Whether there is anything practical or even moral in writing music inspired or provoked by such scenes is another matter. That's the big question. But certainly what we're seeing is the Crucifixion made manifest in our times.

It does come very close sometimes. People walk by your window and you're aware of their suffering. Maybe not in the same degree, but there is great sadness in the eyes of people in our streets. The Crucifixion is manifest in everyone's life at some point.

I don't know that I would write a piece specifically about Kosovo. But the sense of empathy, the sense of compassion, hopefully, the sense of wanting to bring an end to suffering, to bring a redemption, a resurrection, through what is for them crucifixion, is, I think, part of the Christian artist's instincts.

I have enjoyed listening to your music, but although at times I have found myself almost seduced by it, at other times I have found it dissonant and difficult, and it has distanced me. Is that your intention?

It's just the way it comes out. I am drawn to extremes, and to extremes facing each other within the time frame of a piece of music. All the best stories have extreme situations, extreme people, extreme choices, sometimes for good and sometimes for ill. I can't have one without the other.

Some people would say your music is quite élitist, because it can be difficult – and yet you have talked about the importance of music being accessible to everyone. Does that frustrate you?

I feel deeply frustrated sometimes with a culture in which a certain type of music is deemed for this class and another kind is for this class. As someone who comes from a working-class background I was lucky enough to get access to, let's call it the most complex music. Classical music has its complexities in a way that popular music does not, because it doesn't need to. The intentions of serious music, classical music – whatever – are more complicated, I suppose.

To engage with it requires a kind of active hearing, as I was saying earlier. And there are cultural pressures on us not to have that kind of engagement, so that more and more the 'serious' arts are becoming peripheralized. It's not just a musical issue: you find it in literature as well. Reading is under attack from popular culture. Learning could be said to be under attack from popular culture.

So, you see popular culture in very negative terms.

Not always, no. I played in a rock band when I was in my teens. I have certain interests in vernacular musics, if you like. But the ubiquity of popular culture is deeply damaging, because it means that a lot of people, especially from backgrounds like mine, are not getting the opportunities to get a bigger picture. Their options are being limited.

Now, that's not élitism. It's all about rights of access and freedom of opportunity. I see it as a political thing. As a man of the left, I would argue for a greater engagement with all the serious arts, in a way that at present is not possible for whatever reasons. And the power of popular culture is one of them.

How are you trying to make your art more available?

I do a lot of work with orchestras in schools, working in communities that don't normally get access to this kind of music. And that's a kind of spadework which has to be done if there is going to be an audience at all in the future.

The music itself is a different issue. The whole question of accessibility is a complex one. Whereas I would hope that my music is fluent, fluid, powerful enough to communicate, I would never want to think of myself as trying to be populist – writing in order to manipulate emotions, in order to be loved. I think, once a composer starts playing to the gallery he's on a slippy slope.

Obviously, I do write to communicate. I don't think of an audience – I don't think you can: every audience is made up of individuals, and there are some who love certain things and there are others who will loathe them. What I have in mind is an ideal listener – somebody who is as hungry and thirsty for musical experience as I am, who has all antennae bristling and an openness of heart and of mind and a joy in expanding your experience.

Now, audiences are not really like that in the real world, because there's a museum-culture aspect to classical music. People know what they like and like what they know and that's the end of it; and sometimes it's very difficult with that kind of audience to make inroads. But as long as you maintain an integrity, or even an obsessiveness, about your reason for writing, I think it'll get through.

It's not a question of taste. If you remain true to the vision and quest of what you are doing, I think you will communicate regardless, and in some quite surprising circumstances. People who didn't think they would be transformed or opened end up being so. I've seen that in my experience.

I have a feeling that, although I deal with sounds pure and simply, they nevertheless have deeper resonances in our minds, in our psychology, in our corporeality, in our sensual selves. There is a deep connectedness between music and what it means to be human, and so music is not a remote, abstract thing. It does encapsulate something of the narrative of human life. It's not real storytelling, but it has its own drama which somehow, sometimes, reflects the real drama of everyday life and of our history and our politics.

In earlier centuries, the church acted as a patron to many artists. Should it be doing the same now?

It's an interesting point. I think times have changed irrevocably in the sense that the church's relationship with the leading artists has been broken. Its liturgical requirements are no longer the requirements of the community of artists – even Christian artists like myself. My main purpose is not to write music for the liturgy (though I do sometimes): my work exists in a different environment, in the theologically neutral space of the concert hall or the theatre or the opera house, where many different types of people encounter it – non-believers as well as believers, with different understandings of the world and of the nature of humanity and God.

And my music has a natural home in that environment, and has something to say to people who do not share my worldview. That's the power of music. And so to take a step back to what the church did 300, 400 years ago would be wrong. It would narrow the options of the Christian artist, and the Christian artist doesn't want to be narrowed.

However, in wider terms, I think the church has an input into the debate about the arts, and perhaps there is a role for the artist. Whether he's a real believer or someone who floats between ideas, he ought to feel a dialogue and a mutual respect between himself and the worldview of the church. I think that artists, whether they like it or not (and regardless of what they say they believe) are sensors to the divine, and the church should be aware of this and should be monitoring what they are saying. An understanding of living artists should be a priority for theologians, and even for clergy and lay people. An understanding and a respect.

Does it bother you that you have a sacred intention or vision in mind when you're composing, but when the piece is performed in that 'theologically neutral space', listeners can give it a completely different meaning to the one you intended?

I wonder if it is, actually. I think I am specific enough to let people know where the music has come from, and generally people who love the arts are very pluralistic and open-minded – generally – and they tend to respect an artist's inspiration.

However, my music sometimes attracts criticism from a radical-atheistic point of view – and you certainly find that in the world of the arts more and more – which can see in it (quite wrongly) a tendency to proselytize. It's certainly not my role to proselytize at all. To bear witness to what I believe is the truth, certainly – to the source of the music.

> Regardless of what they believe, artists are sensors to the divine. The church should be monitoring what they are saying

It comes through the channel of my own Christian Catholic upbringing and teaching, and the narrowness of that channel perhaps can be quite liberating. That contradicts the notion which is current in the arts, that non-belief is the liberating factor, that freedom of expression goes hand in hand with atheism. It's not necessarily so.

You have talked about your religion and your politics. How important is it to you as a composer, finally, that you are Scottish?

I'm very proud to have been asked to write two fanfares for the official opening of the Scottish Parliament. But I don't think that being Scottish is a big issue when it comes to the music itself. Probably it is flavoured, or even provoked, by my own experiences as a Scot; but if it goes to the other side of the world I don't think people say, 'Oh yes, that sounds Scottish.'

But to be taken seriously, to be respected and celebrated by one's own countrymen is a great joy, and whenever I feel that people are proud of me in Scotland, that does warm my heart.

BIOGRAPHY

James MacMillan was born in 1959 and educated at Cumnock Academy. He read music at Edinburgh and for his doctorate studied composition at Durham University under John Casken.

From 1986 to 1988, he lectured at Manchester University. Since 1989, he has lived in Glasgow and taught part-time at the Royal Scottish Academy of Music and Drama.

In 1990, after the première of *Tryst* at the St Magnus Festival in Orkney, he was appointed affiliate composer of the Scottish Chamber Orchestra. He is artistic director of the Philharmonia Orchestra's Music of Today series of contemporary music concerts, and the Royal Scottish National

Orchestra's Discovery series of twentieth-century music. He is internationally active as a conductor and joined the BBC Philharmonic in September 2000 as its new composer/conductor.

His international career was launched by *The Confession of Isobel Gowdie* at the 1990 BBC Proms. In 1992, he composed for Evelyn Glennie the percussion concerto *Veni, Veni, Emmanuel*, which has received over 200 performances worldwide.

In 1993, the trumpet concerto *Epiclesis* was premièred by the Philharmonia at the Edinburgh Festival and the Koch Schwann recording of *Isobel Gowdie* and *Tryst* won the *Gramophone* Award for contemporary music record of the year.

A year later, his *Seven Last Words from the Cross* for chorus and string orchestra was broadcast by BBC2 during Holy Week and the BMG recording of *Veni, Veni, Emmanuel* won the Classic CD award for contemporary music.

In 1996, *Inés de Castro* was premièred by Scottish Opera at the Edinburgh Festival. In 1997, *Ninian* was performed at the Bergen Festival, and the South Bank and Barbican Centres in London presented a festival of his music, entitled 'Raising Sparks'.

Other major compositions include *Busquéda* (1988), the clarinet quintet *Tuireadh* (1991), the overture *Britannia* (1995), the concerto for cor anglais *The World's Ransoming* and a cello concerto written for Mstislav Rostropovich (both 1996), the clarinet concerto *Ninian*, *Fourteen Little Pictures* for piano trio, *Symphony: Vigil* (whose première Rostropovich conducted), *Raising Sparks* for mezzo-soprano and ensemble (all 1997), and his second string quartet, *Why Is This Night Different?* (1998). *Quickening* (1999), composed for the Hilliard Ensemble, chorus and orchestra, was co-commissioned by the BBC Proms and the Philadelphia Orchestra. MacMillan's most recent orchestral work is *Symphony No. 2*, commissioned by the Scottish Chamber Orchestra and premièred in December 1999.

Future commissions include a music theatre work on the theme of parthenogenesis and orchestral works for the BBC Philharmonic and Los Angeles Philharmonic.

A new series of recordings is under way on the BIS label: releases include *Triduum*, *Ninian* and *Epiclesis*.

He has received honorary doctorates from Paisley and Strathclyde Universities, and is a fellow of the RSAMD.

He has been married since 1983 and has two children. He lists his recreations in *Who's Who* as fatherhood and Celtic FC.

This interview was conducted at James MacMillan's home on 14 May 1999.

Jolyon Mitchell lectures in communication and theology at New College, Edinburgh. He was previously a producer with the BBC World Service. His book *Visually Speaking: Radio and the Renaissance of Preaching* was published by T&T Clark in the autumn of 1999.

ENGAGING IN REFLECTION

Brian Draper talks to author and
observer of a generation,
Douglas Coupland

Your novel _Polaroids from the Dead_ talks of redemption. Do you think we need it – and if so, where do we get it from?

I don't know how you define redemption, but I think yes, we do need it. But how you go about that . . . Boy! Not everyone's a Gandhi, are they?

In a very broad sense, my own perception of redemption involves setting a good example with my life. I think reflection is an important dimension of it. I think that making the time for reflection is . . .

Is redemption a personal project, then, or is there something transcendent we need to connect with?

My next novel (which I finished yesterday) is largely about this issue. So many people are trying to find self-fulfilment through whatever they do in life, but that's just thinking about yourself and doesn't take into account anything larger. Anything you do just for yourself can only end up smaller in some way.

You have to live your life on a few levels. One is the day-to-day. There's another level at which you look at your desires in the framework of eternity: What is the impact of my actions in the long run? Is there something higher or more noble about what I am doing or what I know? What did I do to improve it? _Can_ I improve it?

> You have to look at your desires in the framework of eternity: What is the impact of my actions in the long run?

What do you make of what the Bible says?

I have a friend in New York called Jacob. I ask him, 'Jacob, Jewish people don't believe in the New Testament, is that correct?'

He goes, 'Yeah.'

'But wait, that means there's no redemption.'

He says, 'We believe you live on only through your deeds.'

This sort of thinking goes completely against my intuitive feeling of there being some kind of afterlife – or *something*.

You have described the soul as a twinkle of light that hovers just outside 'the meat', the body. Christians believe in a bodily resurrection –

This is news to me. I thought Jesus was the only one that got resurrected. I had no idea it was everybody. What happens? You get your body back?

Well, the Bible talks of an afterlife and it's not just a disembodied one.

Does it give any details? Are there clouds, or a castle?

No, it's not a fairytale image. Christians believe that creation will be renewed, just as we hope to be.

You often talk of retreating to a primeval world. Do you think we need to recover our original state, rather than holding on to the idea of progress?

An earthly utopia as opposed to heaven? Look at it this way. If you were to take all 5.5 billion people on earth and wave a wand and, suddenly, ping! everybody's at peace, an hour later they'd be squabbling again. I think one's utopia is in one's head – I don't think there's an earthly utopia.

Whatever your situation might be, I think everyone is striving for some sort of purity, some kind of order.

The new hope for eternity is through cryogenics, isn't it, and maybe cloning now?

My brother just made me executor of his will. I said, 'Oh,

you don't want to be cremated, you want to be *embalmed*?' And he said, 'Absolutely – in case they can bring people back from the dead with DNA. I want to have some of that ready for them.' That was two weeks before cloning hit the news.

Suppose they clone you in the year 2050. If I met you both at the shopping mall, how would I tell who was Doug Number One?

In my next book, I have one character from a really churchy family, and he's being a bit too sententious and too right-eous and parroting words without really knowing what he's saying. And, suddenly, there's two of him, and each of them thinks that they're the original.

It's kind of fun for a while – and then an angel comes down and says, 'Oh, there's only room for one of you.' Sud-denly, they have to kill each other. So, they go on this mad hiding-and-killing spree, but the thing is, they both think exactly the same way and so each of them thinks he's found a cool hiding spot – but, of course, the other one finds it at the same time.

There's been a lot of argument about how: you can clone a body but you can't clone a soul. How do we know that? It's all just speculation. We won't know until someone does it. And it's going to happen. You know how we people are: there's some new technology around, people mess with it. Probably within five or ten years.

Is there a common denominator to who you are at different times of your life?

I've asked a lot of people this and everyone seems to agree: 'I was born and around five or six I started having mem-ories and I can't remember ever not feeling like myself.' As you grow older, your perceptions change and you can get more pointed in various specific directions; but you still feel exactly like you. I don't think that ever changes.

And yet your own observation is that our culture has lost its sense of story, both corporate and individual. Do we really end up living life in the present as a series, as you say, of 'interconnected cool moments'?

In New York, a magazine called *Details* is reconfiguring itself as a magazine for young people about work. They say there is no counterculture out there to present. What that says to me is that the culture is all about work: work, work, work, work, work. And if you have any time for reflection at all after that, it's taken up by more work – or exhaustion.

This is where so many people's personal story gets lost, I think. That's the reason that people are going astray: it's not through any wilful act of straying, they're just trying to keep their heads above water financially. That gets overlooked a lot. Everyone says, 'Oh, it's the times we live in – people are selfish.' No, they're not: they're just working.

In the Eighties, there were isolated cool moments; now, I think, we only have uncool moments. Period. People don't have enough time any more to think things through. The biggest luxury now is time to reflect. I consider myself lucky in that way – but then my job is to put my reflections on paper. I go through life trying to do as much reflection as is possible in this culture.

I don't know what it's like in England, but here in Canada nobody has free time any more. Things like arts and crafts and hobbies seem to have vanished. And then when people go to sleep at night they figure they have to spend eight hours working out their problems. That's so sick! Life is all work.

I always find it strange that people spend a third of their lives sleeping and almost none of their lives trying to figure out why.

Everyone says, 'It's the times we live in – people are selfish.' No, they're not, they're just working

You talk about the need to become 'renarrated', to 'get a life'. Doesn't that mean that life becomes just another commodity?

Life does just become another commodity, yes, and I don't think that's good. At this stage of capitalism, life's components are certainly rendered into price-pointed activities. All your needs – even some you didn't even know you had – are taken from you and then sold back to you in some reified form.

Is there any hope for the poor when to have a life you have to buy it? How can they 'choose to live'?

It's a kind of no-win situation. People who have a lot of clock-time on their hands, like the chronically unemployed, are probably not enjoying it, because they're worried about where they get the next meal from. I don't think you find anyone who lives a life of leisure, at any level of society, any more. If they're urban, they're frantic. If they're middle-aged and have kids and stuff, they're wrapped up in that. If they're older, like 60, 70, they're trying to prepare in some way for the end that's ahead. I don't think I've ever met anyone who lives a life of leisure and pleasure. Have you?

One of the most chilling moments in the movie *Train-spotting* is at the very end: he says, 'Get a job, get a haircut and then I'll be just like you.' You realize, 'OK, this guy is still screwed up on smack or whatever, but at least that was interesting. Now he's going to stop being interesting.'

Is there such a thing as a culture of despair?

An entire culture in a state of despair? No. But certainly there are phases in life in which a citizen is slated for unavoidable hard-core despair – usually in the mid-twenties, the early thirties. It usually lasts a year or so. It makes you empathetic to the plight of suffering unseen by the protective device of youthful blitheness.

Some people emerge from this despair with the worry that they're perhaps becoming bitter. It scares you. Even worse: 'Nothing is working out, and going shopping is not going to make me feel any better.' I think that's a point that everybody reaches somewhere in life. I don't think there's one person who's ever lived who didn't say, 'This isn't working. I need something else.'

This is where religion enters. Me, I come from a completely secular household and a completely secular neighbourhood and I can't imagine what it'd be like to have been raised in a family with church and religious trappings. When you get stuff that young, I think, it always comes back to you when you're older.

But a culture of despair – I think the despairing now is probably over jobs and the economy. You have to live in this world; you have to pay the rent. Ironically, metaphysical issues are on the backburner at the exact point when they should be up front.

In *Life after God*, the narrator admits that he is sick and needs God. Why does he?

I think that goes back to what I was saying about how you can live your life solely for yourself and have self-fulfilment and happiness, or you can live your life according to some transcendent values, or with a code of ethics that gives you foundations to stand on.

It's extraordinarily difficult, if not impossible, to build a religion on your own. (How many religions are there? Twenty?) Jenny Holzer says, 'Many things are decided before you are born,' which is quite true. If religion is part of your culture, your society, your community, and you like living in that milieu, then there's something to it and you should maybe have a look at it.

What do you need God for: to dull the pain or heighten the pleasure?

Neither. I think it's more that six days out of seven you go to work, or you're taking care of the kids or whatever your life is, and very few people can say, 'Today I developed the Theory of Relativity,' or 'I've just written this song.' Most people at the end of the day just have to say, 'I lived my life.'

And that's fine, but it's kind of scary, too, when your life seems small or you don't think you're doing anything worthy. I think religion is important because it makes you

Ironically, meta-physical issues are on the back-burner exactly when they should be up front

feel that even if your day seems like it was small, it was big and you did something worthy. Even though you didn't write a song or invent a theory, you did make some kind of metaphysical bridge or window.

Are you suggesting in your books that people are looking for transcendence?
Primarily transcendence and epiphany, yes.

What would you ask Christ if he showed up unexpectedly?
That's personal. It would be between only us.

Suppose God invited you to an end-of-the-world party and it was fancy dress. Who would you go as?
Either Abraham Lincoln or Vaclav Havel, because they both have a lucidity of thought that is so rare that when you find it, you treasure it. Dressing like them would be a way of saying, 'OK, the world's over, but look, there were some good things about it as well as bad.'

If culture is the means by which we process reality, wouldn't it be more harmonious and efficient if the whole world had the same culture?
It sounds good in theory, but in practice it stinks. Imagine going to a party where everyone was exactly the same! Whoooeeee! I wonder if the world would be more harmonious if every single soul was both confident and eccentric . . . Good luck!

I'm always suspicious of people who rely on their ethnicity, beliefs, hair colour or what have you as a major part of their identity. Like, don't you have anything else going for you?

Memory and nostalgia permeate your books –
I think nostalgia is simply memory looked at with sentiment.

Does video distort human memory? A friend of mine told me that her recollection of her wedding day was completely different from the video – which she enjoyed much more.

When you go to a dinner party, the chef very rarely sits down at the table. He or she has maybe a glass of wine and then they're back in the kitchen. And they rarely eat because they're too busy making sure everyone else is having a good time. But 20 years on your friend will think, 'What a beautiful wedding it was, as I remember it.' Except, now she doesn't have to wait 20 years. Video accelerates that memory. That's OK. It was going to happen anyway, so it may as well happen now.

What, for you, makes a good story?

It has to be set after 1920, for then people had telephones and cars and plots become accelerated and more varied.

What do you think of the Bible as a story?

I like the New Testament much more than the Old, probably because it has more narrative.

I worked briefly in magazines, and a story would come in and then everyone would give it a read and everybody would tamper with it and in the end there was a great big muddle. Which is not to say that the Bible's a muddle; but don't we all just know that a ton of material has been taken out of it, to suit whatever agenda was popular at whatever time in history? It's been so really heavily edited – dozens, if not hundreds, of times. It's distracting.

In *Life after God*, you suggest that there are just a few things that differentiate us from animals, such as writing and smoking. Do you think it odd that we are the only species that wears clothes?

I've never thought of that before. Yes, it's bizarre.

The issue gets scrambled when it comes to cartoons: in

some shots, Donald Duck is wearing pants and in some he's not wearing anything. So, are those naughty shots?

When you get dressed, are you covering up who you are or becoming who you are?

I have such a strange relationship with the body. I was pencil-thin up until about 31, 32, and decided I'd had enough of that, so I ate properly and went to the gym and I now have a body. But I can't wear any of my old clothes any more. The fact that at the moment I'm wearing gym clothes, I guess, is reflective of who I am becoming.

The US painter Georgia O'Keeffe used to wear only black and white and when asked why, her answer was: 'I have to put all my colour energy into my painting; I don't have to think about colour in the morning when I'm putting on clothes.'

In the Genesis story, God gave Adam and Eve clothes after their relationship with him was damaged, because they felt shame. Today, it seems we wear them either to cover up or to reinvent ourselves.

I think most people wear clothes to amplify their good bits and hide their not-so-good bits. As a culture, our naughty bits are all covered.

Heavy-duty experimentation with clothing and style tends to happen in arenas where there's a religious vacuum – in youth culture, or places like Los Angeles, which is a city entirely estranged from its conception as a Protestant metropolitan utopia. I also notice that most people are estranged from religion from about 17 to 27, and I've noticed that the need to keep up with the latest fashion and whatever is something that happens in your twenties.

> I think sin has to be recalibrated: there's no real scale of one to ten. If you do one thing wrong, you're screwed for eternity

If we couldn't see what we looked like, would it affect our humanity? I wonder what the mirror has done for our understanding of who we are.

I've actually been trying to research when mirrors were invented. The first people who had good mirrors, not just little tiny reflective things, were the French, I believe. Its influence was enormous. Only the kings and queens were able to see themselves, and their fashion became so ornate and detailed. The aspiring middle classes might have had them, but otherwise no one had mirrors.

Mirrors really are like the wheel of fire: an unbelievably fundamental and transformative object. If no one had mirrors, I suppose you'd never quite know why people were treating you the way they do – because looks, certainly in North America, have a lot to do with the way people treat you. People would walk around wondering why no one looks at them, or why everyone does.

Since Christians believe that we are made in God's image, in theory we ought to be reflecting something of him. Judging by the way we dress and the way we act, what do you think God looks like?

Well, in the States – and in Canada, though not nearly so much – I've noticed that people who are Baptists, 'televangelical' and fundamentalist Christians dress to look as antiseptic and free of orifices as they can. And they put that blue water stuff in the toilet bowl. I don't mean that as a snide comment: that's just what I've noticed. And in their fridges everything is completely orderly. It's as if the more they add order to the universe and to themselves, the closer they are to the Christian God.

I don't know. I don't think God's dressed like these people. I don't think he's wearing a three-piece suit.

What advice would you give the church to make its story more accessible?

I'm not the best person to ask – I've been in a church once, for a friend's wedding. But, off the top of my head, I think sin has to be recalibrated. There's no real scale of one to ten: if you do one thing wrong, you're screwed for eternity. Atonement should more closely relate to the transgression.

The future and the afterlife are two different things

altogether: if someone dumps toxic waste in a pond and then dies, it's like, 'Ha ha! I got off easy.' I think there has to be some 'Uh uh, you have to pay for that.' Our role on earth is partly to shepherd Nature, and keeping the world clean is fundamental. There's no ecological dimension in any religion and I think that's just pathetic.

And I think religion should probably try to find a bit more fusion with the economy, the way people actually have to live their lives, and connect with the way work is going.

Wow! These are some of the best questions I've ever had. I hope I've been answering them.

BIOGRAPHY

Douglas Coupland was born on a Nato base in West Germany on the penultimate day of 1961, but he grew up (and still lives) in Vancouver.

He graduated in 1984 from that city's Emily Carr Institute of Art and Design with a degree in sculpture, and then studied fine art and industrial design in Japan at the Hokkaido College of Art and Design Sculpture and in Milan at the European Design Institute. He also holds a degree in Japanese Business Science.

In 1987, he had a solo sculptural installation at the Vancouver Art Gallery, entitled 'The Floating World'.

He is best known as a novelist. His books to date, *Generation X* (1991), *Shampoo Planet* (1992), *Life after God* (1994), *Microserfs* (1995), *Polaroids from the Dead* (1996), *Girlfriend in a Coma* (1998), and *Miss Wyoming* (2000), have been translated into a total of 22 different languages.

He also contributes to the *New York Times*, the *New Republic*, *Wired* and *Wallpaper*.

Douglas Coupland is no longer doing design work, but is an artist in the process of signing up with a gallery.

This interview was conducted over the phone on 11 March 1997.

At the time of the interview Brian Draper was editor of *Third Way*. He now lectures in contemporary culture at the London Institute for Contemporary Christianity. His first book, *Refreshing Worship*, co-written with Kevin Draper, was published by Bible Reading Fellowship in 2000.

THIRD WAY

Third Way is a magazine for people who haven't lost faith in God or lost touch with the world. Since 1977, it has been (as one reader put it) '*a crucial voice in these interesting times, offering rigorous Christian thinking on politics, society and culture*'.

Visit our website at www.thirdway.org.uk to discover who is behind *Third Way* and who reads it. You will also find there a large library of our interviews – from Tony Blair to Ian Hislop – as well as a wealth of other material. And you can order a free sample of the magazine or take out a subscription on-line.

'*One of the best ways I know to engage a hard-thinking faith with the realities of life.*' Michael Taylor, president of Jubilee 2000

Third Way, St Peter's, Sumner Road,
Harrow HA1 4BX, UK
Phone: (+44) (0)20 8423 8494
Fax: (+44) (0)20 8423 5367
e-mail: editor@thirdway.org.uk